James Baker

Pictures from Bohemia

James Baker

Pictures from Bohemia

ISBN/EAN: 9783743463417

Manufactured in Europe, USA, Canada, Australia, Japa

Cover: Foto ©Andreas Hilbeck / pixelio.de

Manufactured and distributed by brebook publishing software (www.brebook.com)

James Baker

Pictures from Bohemia

PICTURES FROM BOHEMIA

Drawn with Pen and Pencil

BY

JAMES BAKER F.R.G.S.

AUTHOR OF 'A GREAT FORGOTTEN ENGLISHMAN' 'MARK TILLOTSON' 'BY THE WESTERN SEA'
'JOHN WESTACOTT' 'DAYS AFOOT' ETC.

WITH A MAP AND ONE HUNDRED AND EIGHT ILLUSTRATIONS

FROM DRAWINGS BY WALTER CRANE H. WHATLEY AND THE BEST BOHEMIAN ARTISTS

JOHN HUS

1894

THE RELIGIOUS TRACT SOCIETY

56 PATERNOSTER ROW AND 65 ST. PAUL'S CHURCHYARD

From a water-colour drawing)   THE TOWN GATE AT PRACHATIC.   *[by Walter Crane.*

From a drawing]   BOHEMIAN BRIDAL COSTUME.   *[by H. Whatley.*

PREFACE.

To travel in Bohemia is to travel in a land full of strange natural beauty, where the people are imbued with an intense love for their historic past, and live a life of centuries ago, blended with an active energy that makes them one of the foremost industrial people of Europe.

Cross through the passes that alone lend access to this mountain-locked land, and one is in a land of romance almost unknown to the British tourist. Hitherto the travellers who have visited Bohemia have been the seekers after health, who have gone to her famous baths lying on her borders, such as Teplitz, Carlsbad, and Marienbad; or those who have visited her famous capital, Prague; or the business-men who have gone to her commercial centres, such as Gablonz. Yet these have seen but little of Bohemia and her people, for in her baths and capital she is cosmopolitan, and but little of the real life of her people is there seen.

It is in her villages and lesser towns that custom and costume still survive of past centuries; and it is in her mountain recesses that castle, and monastery, and mediæval towns, full of a strange past glory, are to be studied. And it is in her mountains also that are seen the weird scenes of her rock towns, unsurpassed in Europe for wild savage grandeur. Her history speaks forth in the innumerable ruins of her castles that crown her mountain peaks, or hide amidst the secret passes of these natural rock towns; or in the beautiful architecture of such a church as that of St. Barbara at Kuttenberg, or 'Kutna Hora,' as the Bohemians term it.

Bohemia, with the above exceptions, is still an unknown land, and the English traveller who wanders amidst its small towns and villages could give curious items of the wonder and surprise of the inhabitants at the sight of an Englishman, even as strange as those of the more distant traveller who penetrates into the far east of Asia; and yet in the Middle Ages Bohemia exercised a mighty influence in European life. It is in a large degree to the noble teaching and martyr death of John Hus, and in lesser measure to the sturdy Hussite warriors in their linked waggon forts that Europe owes soul freedom. And a tour within her borders gives an insight into the passionate life of her people and offers sights and scenes of mediæval life even to-day, that carry one back into feudal times.

The costumes of her peasants on *fête* days is still the most vividly brilliant in Europe. Their love of music adds greatly to the pleasure of wandering amongst them, and a tour in Bohemia becomes a series of pleasant though ofttimes startling surprises, so sharp are the contrasts of life, and so sudden are the changes of scenery, theatrical yet fascinating. The historian and archæologian, the geologist, musician, artist, and technologist will find much to study in Bohemia, and the tourist who travels even without a special aim, becomes deeply interested in the scenery and people and mediæval remains. Through these 'Pen and Pencil Pictures' we hope to interest many in her life of to-day, and to give some glimpses into the pleasure of wandering within Bohemia's mountain borders.

A VIEW AT BÖHMISCH LEIPA.

CONTENTS AND LIST OF ILLUSTRATIONS.

CHAPTER I.

THE GATEWAY INTO BOHEMIA.

CHAPTER II.

THE CASTLES OF BURGSTEIN, RALSKO, AND BÖSIG.

CHAPTER III.

FRIEDLAND, GABLONZ, AND TURNAU.

CHAPTER IV.

JICIN AND ITS SURROUNDINGS.

CHAPTER V.

KUTTENBERG AND ITS ASSOCIATIONS.

CHAPTER VI.

PRAGUE.

CHAPTER XI.

SAAZ AND THE ELBE.

ERRATA.

In Chapter II. . . *for* Rolsko *read* Ralsko.
On page 40, line 31, „ Great „ Giant.
„ 45, „ 7, „ Scratched „ Serrated.
„ 46, „ 37, „ Waldenstein „ Wallenstein.
„ 63, under cut, „ Castle „ Barracks.

On page 64, under cut, *for* Barrack *read* Stone House.
„ 66, „ „ Jacobi „ Barbara.
„ 68, line 9, „ Shillings „ Groschen.
„ 113, under cut, „ Gipsies „ Peasants.

From a drawing by]   BOHEMIAN MUSICIANS.   *[H. Whatley.*

VIEW OF PILSEN

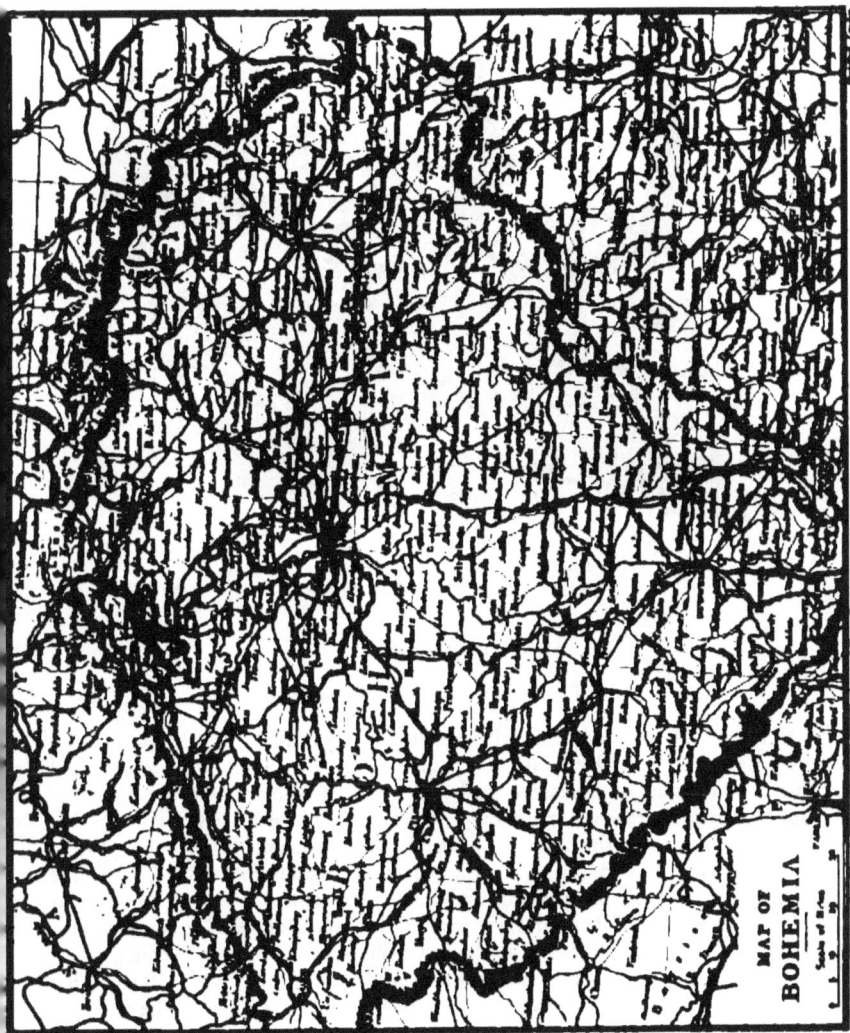

MAP OF
BOHEMIA

Scale of Miles

From a drawing]   GROTESQUE ROCK PILLAR AT ADERSBACH.   *[by H. Whatley.*

CHAPTER I.

THE GATEWAY INTO BOHEMIA.

THE most pleasant mode of entering into Bohemia from England is by way of the Elbe; take the steamer to the Hook of Holland, and thence by train to Dresden, and from this Saxon capital the gates of Bohemia can be reached by, perhaps, the most picturesque river journey that Europe has to offer the traveller. The Elbe is ascended betwixt the gigantic natural fortresses and fantastic rock pillars of Saxon Switzerland, until the frontier of Saxony is passed, and one alights upon Bohemian soil at Herrenskretchen. When first we visited this spot, descending to it from a walk over the mountain passes in the soft twilight of an autumn evening, it was but a village with a little two-storied inn, facing the broad Elbe. That was in 1873; and like many another tourist we knew nought of the wonders,

natural and artistic, of the land we had entered. But as in after years visit
succeeded visit to Bohemia, its endless succession of natural wonders, and
exciting historic episodes, developed themselves slowly, and with ever increasing charm and interest; and it is thus in this volume we would strive to
let a knowledge of
Bohemia, the coun-
try, the people, and
their history, grow
upon the reader.

As scene succeeds
scene, and picture
follows picture, so
peeps into her past
history will present
themselves, as we
stand upon the
spots where the
deeds that made his-
tory were enacted.
No romance written
ever evolved from an
imaginative brain,
facts so terrible or
strange as may be
read in the fiery his-
tory of the land of
Hus; and no novelist
ever laid the plot of
his story in scenes
so romantic as those
we shall have to de-
scribe, and at Herren-
skretchen this
romantic beauty
commences.   When
last we halted here,
it had grown into a
small town, and the
two-storied inn had

ROCK SCENERY ON THE ELBE.

developed into a four-storied hotel ; but above its four stories towered the rocks
that form the gateway of the pass up the little river, and soon away up this
pass we walked ; and in ten minutes we had crossed the small rushing torrent
stream, and were alone amidst the pines and rock pillars, with no sound but

of the rushing waters and the trickling brooklets, hastening down to join the greater stream. The strange suggestive sound of the wind in the pines called up visions of the sea even in mid Europe, so like the rush and sighing of waters on the beach is this soughing of the winds through the pine branches.

We went on up the steep ascent, passing the first of the strange lovely, yet picturesque little cemeteries on the mountain side, of which we were to see so many in such strange situations throughout Bohemia, and soon reached the village of Johnsdorf. From the open plateau above this village is a wide-stretching view of the country around, with its mountain ranges and isolated peaks, and tablelands all fresh now with the young foliage of spring.

Through a wonderful mass of rock piers we descended upon slippery ice-clad paths, until the level of the little River Kamnitz that flows into the Elbe at Herrenskretchen was reached; and here on a bridge that spanned its rushing tumultuous waters we looked round on a scene of intense beauty.

Down by the side of the tumultuous river we started to walk, for it reached Herrenskretchen, and the possessor of the property, Prince Clary, had lately hewn a path beside the waters that enabled foot passengers to follow the river's course; but Nature had in one spot thrown two great obstacles in the way by a sheer precipice of rock on either side of the river. To talk of a boat on this tumbling, roaring, spring-flushed torrent, seemed absurd; but as we neared the spot, passing under mighty piers and walls of rock, the sound of waters lessened; and as we gained the place where the path ends, the river has worn a deep bed for itself between the rock walls, and moves silently onward. A block-house has been set up in an opening in the rocks, and here a boat is found to take the pedestrian on between the rock walls, to where the path again commences by the river's bank.

How strange it was to embark with only the steersman in the rude boat upon the deep, dark waters, knowing the force of torrent that was rushing on above us, to float in the intense silence into the dark gorge, with rocks some two to three hundred feet high shutting in all sight, save above, the slit of deep blue sky. The rocks all worn and eaten, but clothed with the brilliant sulphur lichen, or moss clad; and great pines topped on pines where a cleft in the wall gave hold to the tentacles of the pine roots. Waterfalls came down, some still pure ice, in white cascades. In one spot a great sheet of ice was lying over a great mass of rock, like some giants' table-cloth; and the silence and weirdness of the scene made one expect to see Gnome or Pixie moving in the rock clefts. Softly and silently the waters bore us on through the gorge, until ahead we heard the distant softened rush of a cataract; but so changing was the scene of widening rocks and opening amphitheatres all filled with pine columns, and succeeding these again a narrowing of the stream, that the ominous roar of waters was forgotten until its increasing strength made us look anxiously at the steersman. He reassured us there was no danger; and as we drew near, we saw beneath an overhanging mass of rock some 150 feet high a little landing-place; and here we left the boat, but we lingered long in the scene around us, for it was strangely wild and romantic.

There is another famous spot that lies within the Bohemian frontier, and is within easy walking distance of Herrenskretchen, that few will care to miss; for it gives a sight of one of Nature's strangest freaks and most grandiose effects. The road to this trends back towards the Saxon frontier, and is but just inside the boundary-line, but the famous Prebischthor is on Bohemian earth. The walk to the Prebischthor is in summer at least fairly frequented, as it is one of the great sights of this favourite district. After mounting up with dark grey rock walls on either hand, between which the pines go up tall, straight, majestic, we reach the great isolated pillars of rock and the mighty arch of the Prebischthor. It is a natural bridge, thrown across a span of some hundred feet from the mountain side, to the great natural bastion of worn rock that dives down, far down, into the pine forest below. Steps lead up to the summit of the arch, and as it is broad there is no danger in walking across it; and from the supporting bastion summit a marvellous expanse of view is to be enjoyed.

The steamboat journey from Herrenskretchen to Tetschen is short; and as the suspension bridge of Tetschen comes in sight, the mountains recede from the river, and now a full view into Bohemia can be obtained; for Tetschen can almost be named the Elbe gate of Bohemia. And this the powerful race of the Wartenbergs quickly saw; and early in the fourteenth century they added it to their mountain strongholds, that already dominated so vast a tract of North Bohemia. But Tetschen was of importance before this date, for in 1125 it is mentioned as the chief town of a *zupa* or district.

As the steamer sweeps up to the mooring place, Tetschen gives to the traveller no idea of its antiquity. Even its castle, perched upon a low rock-crag some slight distance from the river, looks new and not more than two centuries old in any part of it. But both town and castle have much of interest, and like the scenery we have just passed through, are a gentle and pleasant preparation for stronger and more exciting strongholds, and more mediæval towns.

The castle that was held by the Wartenbergs for two hundred years is now in the possession of the powerful race of the Thuns; and for two hundred years from 1670, the burial-place of this family was in the Loretto Chapel in the market-place, Count Max Thun in 1691 having also built for the town the Kreuzkirche and decorated it with frescoes. A stroll round to the back of the castle grounds, and over the little bridge, up the long rock-hewn avenue, leads into the castle garden, where is a famous rosary boasting of some two thousand varieties of roses. The inner courtyard is, however, almost the only part of the building that carries one back into the past life of Bohemia, though situated as it was on the frontier of the kingdom, Tetschen suffered severely in the Hussite and seventeenth and eighteenth century wars.

So long as we linger near the banks of the Elbe, we are amid a Teutonic and German-speaking race. Rivers have always been the great

TETSCHEN CASTLE AND BRIDGE.

highways along which invading races have penetrated slowly into other lands, and on the Elbe banks but little of the true Bohemian character is met with.

The love of vivid colour is not noticeable in the dress of the peasants ; the passionate gaiety and love of music and dramatic representations is not so marked ; the fair-haired race predominates, and the dark-haired eastern type of face of the Cech is more rarely met with, and German is almost exclusively spoken. But at Tetschen we leave the glorious Elbe stream, to again revisit it later on, and ascend by one of the small new mountain railways into the busy mountainous districts of Northern Bohemia. Soon the line begins to ascend, twisting and twining amidst meadows and mountain streams, and in spring time numerous waterfalls.

HAIDA.

Soon after the top of the pass is reached, and the train runs down to Haida, our next halting-place. Haida is not a fashionable resort. The tourist who longs for an afternoon promenade, and a *table-d'hôte* dinner, will not find them here. The inn is a building with very solid walls, and vaulted roof, and a gateway to the stairs, very suggestive of a prison; but on ascending these stairs the bedrooms are found to be perfectly clean, with spotless sheets, and none of the filth that is to be met with in Italian or French country inns in unvisited spots ; and in many of these Bohemian hostelries the cooking is excellent ; and in some the guests are shown through the kitchens to the dining-rooms, that all the cleanliness of the *batterie de cuisine* may be seen, and commented upon.

One can be very comfortable at the Eagle at Haida, and it is an excellent centre for some of the most strange and interesting excursions in Bohemia. Carriages can be hired with good horses at reasonable rates, though hardly so cheaply as in some other parts of the country, where ten shillings for a day's drive with two horses and a man is the general tariff.

A DOORWAY AT BOHMISH LEIPA.

THE CHAPEL, BÖSIG CASTLE.

CHAPTER II.

THE CASTLES OF BURGSTEIN, ROLSKO, AND BÖSIG.

HAIDA is a well-ordered, busy, clean town, with long roads, bordered on either hand with well-to-do villas, stretching away from the central square, where is an excellent technical school, the church and town-hall and fountain, a wide open tank of water fed by the mountain spring. All around rise up the pine heights of the mountains; and glorious walks are within easy distance. On a Sunday or *fête* day the scene in the white-

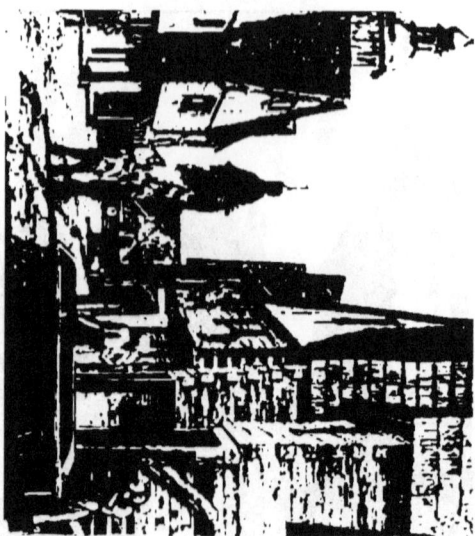

towered, red-domed church is most striking.   On the left hand are the women, a blaze of colour, for every woman wears a head-dress of brilliant hues : every shade and every combination of colour is there, red, blue, brown, yellow, black, sky blue, crimson, green, grey, violet, ultramarine, orange : but as the German element is here largely intermixed, the women's dresses are not of the same gorgeous hues as may be seen in the purely Cech districts. The singing in the church is good, and a full string band is accompanied by a good organ. Gay banners are hung round the chancel, and Haida being the centre of the glass trade, the gaseliers with glass pendants are very rich, and glitter in the light. On the one side of the church no operatic scene could be more full of colour ; but on the men's side all is dark, grey, and sombre, for they wear here modern costume *sans* bright hues. As the women's voices rise up in rich full notes, and the trumpets and organ burst forth in powerful harmony, it is hard to believe that this is a church in a small town of Bohemia.

Within an easy walk is the strange rock castle of Burgstein.   We visited it one fine spring morning, and were soon away from all glimpses of town life, and amidst the silent forest, yet not wholly silent, for the wind sighed through the dark pines that shaded us from the hot sun. Soon we emerged on a fruit-tree bordered road, and ahead was a village ; and in a level meadow plain rose up a great isolated block of rock. The mountain spurs were some distance from it, it rose alone, an enormous mass of yellow sandstone apparently, nought but a natural rock-island crowned with firs. But on obtaining from a house near some keys, we were admitted into the heart of this rock, and found it to be a perfect castle with chambers and chapel, stables and halls, all scooped laboriously out of the living rock. The principal entrance to it was a V-shaped narrow stairway, up which only one person at a time could ascend ; and this arrangement we met with in other famous robber-knights' strongholds. Like all Bohemian castles it had its Hunger Tower, but this one had been cut open, and on its walls were carved in this great silent rock-dungeon roses and crosses, a death dance, a woman with a child, numerous death's heads, and the famous sign of the Hussites, the Chalice. In one spot were a number of strokes, perchance the day-tally of some poor wretch who would fain keep some reckoning of how time sped on.

As this castle is unique, even in Bohemia, in spite of our limited space that compels us only to glance at much upon which many pages might be written, an outline of the history of this fortress must be given ; it is the history of many another robber-nest. When it was first used as a dwelling-place is unknown, but its documentary history begins in 1327 ; in 1426 its then lord was bond for the ransom of some men of Lausitz, who had been captured by the Hussites ; but as some Hussites had also been captured by the Burgstein vassals, the high price of seventy Schock (a *schock* means sixty) of groschen was refused for a batch of the Lausitz prisoners. In the year 1440, Burgstein was in the hands of Mikisch Panzer, who used it as a centre from whence to raid the whole district. So fierce and unbearable did these raids become, that the chief towns near, Zittau, Leipa, and even Breslau and Schweidnitz, combined, and in August completely destroyed it. From that day to this no one has inhabited Burgstein,

BURGSTEIN ROCK CASTLE.

save a hermit, who for many years lived here, and erected calvarys, and carved religious inscriptions on the walls, where robber-knight and men-at-arms had revelled over their deeds of violence and bloodshed.

We descended from this rock, full of wonder at its strangeness, and by a well-made road, lined with short basalt columns, journeyed towards Schwoika, where is another rock fortress, and modern château still inhabited and modernised; but near it is a most strange praying-place of the peasantry. Leaving the main road we entered a thick dark forest, and commenced to ascend. Soon, between the pine-columns, we saw coming down towards us, flitting between the dark aisles of the forest, bright patches of colour; it was a group of children in every hue; soon great masses of rock rose up around us, some hundreds of feet in height, and then in the depth of the pines we saw kneeling before a rock-hewn chapel, lit with many candles, groups of peasants in their bright head-dresses. Most solemnly strange was the scene. The little chapel was well formed, with pillars, and arches, and mouldings, all scooped and worked from the rock; and away on all sides from it went the dark columns of the pines, stretching into positive blackness, so thick was the forest; still higher up the mountain rose some steep wooden steps, and at the top of these was an altar, still surrounded with the winter's snow, that lay in whiteness, contrasting with the brown carpet of the pine spines at lower depths. Up to this solitary forest altar we climbed, and before it knelt a woman in a black velvet jacket and red and white head-dress, and a little child with an intensely red head-dress; but utter stillness was there, a stillness of silence that made the light breath of the wind in the pines audible, and awful in its whispering; and we could, to some extent, realise with what a power this forest praying-place has held the peasantry for centuries past, in spite of Church and changing creed; for it is unconsecrated and unrecognised by the Church.

A glorious day's drive from Haida, full of historical and antiquarian interest, and giving glimpses of village life and wide-spreading wonder-exciting views, is that which takes the robber-knights' castle of Ralsko on the Roll Mountain as its farthest point. The road leads through a minutely cultivated country, where no corner of land is left untilled; the roadside being lined with fruit-trees that in spring fill the air with the scent of the blossom, and in autumn are laden with fruit. Many a hint might our English agriculturist gain from the care, and thought, and economy of the Bohemian small holder: more intensely careful is he than the Belgian agriculturist, who is so often spoken of as the pattern for *petite culture.*

The first place reached on this drive is the historic town of Reichstadt. Its great square schloss or castle is not very picturesque, looking more like a factory than a castle; but a spire and tower adds to its architecture. The timber houses around are more artistic, with their timber pillars supporting the second storey. The name that at once rises on the lips on visiting Reichstadt is that of Napoleon; for from this little far-distant town he gave the title of Duke of Reichstadt to his son, although he himself had never visited it. From Reichstadt the road leads on to Niemes, a spot we shall again halt at upon another drive, and then a by-road leads to the village of Rabensdorf, where at a little inn the carriage can be left, and the ascent of the Roll Mountain made.

An hour's climb brings you to a great scree or slide of basalt débris.

Toiling over this, you reach at last, at the height of some 2100 feet, the first traces of the old robbers' nest. A most extraordinary place it is, perched on a peaked precipice. The arches to the basement were worked with rough-hewn stone, and with no keystone, apparently very early work; but within the walls was a square keep of worked stone, with round embrasures, also of worked stone. From the summit of these battlements we looked forth upon an enormous view. Standing upon this narrow peak, the whole country lay beneath; plain on plain, mountain beyond mountain; villages dotted thickly, and small towns; great forest tracts as black spots,

THE ROLL MOUNTAIN.

and away on the north a pretty little blue lake; whilst to the east rose up a snowy range of mountains, the Giant and the Iser Mountains. Nearer were lesser hills, rounded and cultivated or black with pines.

As the landscape beneath these mountain peaks tempts one to linger on and on, so the history of the old ruined walls carries one back and back into the fierce past, when in the name of religion brother fought brother; many perchance but for power, and might, and wealth; but others earnestly, for freedom to man's soul from fallible power and human thraldom. Fierce stories and wild legends cling around these ruined walls. The history of these castles is the history of that great outbreak of Bohemia under the influence of Wyclif and his great follower Hus that set Europe, nay, the world, free from one Italian overlord ; and if an Englishman was the primary influence that loosened the springs of thought, and sent Hus upon his world-freeing mission, so an Englishman, Peter Payne, was the director and counsellor of these Bohemian Wyclifites, who defied the greatest power the world then knew. And he learnt to know the inner fortresses and dark rock dungeons of these mountain strongholds, and probably often in his journeyings to and fro in this then torn land, he had looked up to this castle-cragged height on the Roll, even if he never rested within its courts. The castle seems to have consisted of outer courts and two square towers and keeps, between which are numerous halls, through which run the ridges of basalt rock. We lingered long on the great rock that abuts on the farthest keep, a sheer precipice some 1200 feet down to the plain beneath. But at length we tore ourselves from view and ruin, and found a fair path down the mountain side.

THE HUNGER TOWER, BÖSIG CASTLE.

From Haida upon another morning we went by train through a lovely country to the little town of Hirschberg, to visit the mighty ruin of Bösig. Hirschberg is also a pleasant halting-place, and here is one of the present castles and residences of the Countess of Waldstein ; but a little farther on the line is the small station of Bezdez or Bösig, and high up on a cone-shaped hill the twin towers of Bosig tempt one up to its height, and when amidst its walls, wonder is excited at what must have been its greatness and grandeur when under the sway of the

famous Wallenstein, to whom Schiller has given immortality. Bosig goes
back to the date of William of Normandy's conquest of England, and its
documentary history dates from 1185. Since that date its walls have

INTERIOR OF CHAPEL, BÖSIG CASTLE.

witnessed varied scenes of grandeur and of horror.   At one time used
as a State prison, at another as the shelter of Queen Kunikunde and the
Crown Prince Wenzel. In the Hussite wars the inflamed and victorious
Taborites surrounded and captured it and set it in flames ; but it was again
rebuilt, to be again destroyed in the seventeenth century. In the year 1622

it came into the hands of the seventh Duke of Friedland, Albert of Wallenstein, who added to its grandeur, and founded here an Augustinian monastery. Then again it fell into the hands of the Crown, and was handed over to the Benedictines, who turned the whole castle into a monastery, set up a statue to the Virgin in the castle chapel, and established a pilgrimage to this castle-crowned height. In 1785 this monastery was closed, and the late warder's grandfather did his work of destruction, until stopped by the Wallensteins, into whose possession it again passed, and Count Christian of Wallenstein restored the great central tower.

Such is the bare skeleton of the history of this strange and picturesque building.[1] The graduated path up which armed knight and hooded dame had ridden on its timber slabs, is now bordered with stations of the cross for the peasant pilgrims who annually still visit the holy height. The three gateways are still there, the last that stands, beyond an awkward mass of basalt slabs piled up to about eighty feet, is in good preservation, and just inside the view of great embattled walls, massive towers, and little chapel is full of beauty. The nearest tower is the great Hunger Tower, a mass of masonry, with walls fifteen feet in thickness. How terrible the secrets hidden within these castles were, we saw on entering the very beautiful little chapel, for at one of the trefoil-headed windows the spaces at the sides had been walled up, and on being opened, one was found empty, while the other contained a skeleton in an upright position. The steps up to the clerestory in this chapel are still accessible, and from here the quality of the work on corbels and mouldings can be examined ; the roof is full of bullets, said to be from the time of the Seven Years' War, but one we extracted was suggestive of a modern rifle bullet, and seemed to say that the 18,000 Prussians who encamped around it in 1866 before Königgrätz, that lies to the east, had not passed on without using their rifles.

A good stairway leads up the great central tower, and from its summit, some 800 feet above the village below, and 2000 feet above the sea-level, a glorious view is spread beneath. Far over the plain rises up the conical mountain. Hirschberg lies beyond the forest with its two blue lakes, made by Carl V. The second line of the Giant Mountains adds a distant beauty to the scene, and even Teplitz and Tetschen and Prague can be sighted with good glasses from this height. Below, the Swedish trenches can still be seen, and the whole vista of landscape and ruin, of chapel and kitchens, Rittersaal and Hunger Tower, bring up pages of history and incident to the mind as we stray on in the warm sunshine on this fascinating height.

We have dwelt upon this castle almost more than space permits, for with Carlstein it is one of the most famous ruins in Bohemia, though we shall visit other castles still inhabited of the same antiquity, and with almost parallel history.

[1] See article on Bosig, by J. B., *Gentleman's Magazine*, April, 1887.

From a drawing]   NIEMES.   [by Walter Crane.

CHAPTER III.

FRIEDLAND, GABLONZ, AND TURNAU.

ANOTHER town in this North Bohemia that makes an excellent halting-place with good accommodation is Turnau, or to give it the Cech spelling, Turnov ; and to reach this from the district we have been exploring, a two days' drive from Niemes is thoroughly enjoyable, embracing a most varied diversity of life and scenery. Here we are getting amidst a Cech population, and the colours worn by the peasantry are more brilliant, especially upon *fête* days. In driving on from Niemes, the town of Wartenberg makes a pleasant halting-place, its castle moat is now a fruit orchard, and the old ruined castle of Dewin upon its rocky height should be visited. The carriage can be left at a little inn, in the village of Hammer, that faces a picturesque cottage with carved timber gables, where Gabriel Max, the famous painter, came into this world ; and from this inn a lovely walk beside a fish-filled lake up amidst the forest leads up to the strange ruin. There is much more left of the architecture of this castle than of the Roll Ralsko ruin. The courtyard, with its solid five-feet thick walls, still remains, and perhaps within it may be met a company of Bohemian or Saxon pleasure-seekers, singing in good harmony some part-song, and making the old walls echo with the clink of glasses and hearty

laughter, for we are close to the Saxon frontier still, and the Cechs point to the Saxon excursionists as foreigners.

The road on to Turnau passes through Oschitz, with its timbered houses, and so on to Böhmisch Aicha, where the night can be passed in a comfortable inn at reasonable rates, though the sleeping guest chambers being limited, the traveller may have to take a bed in one of the great rooms so common to these inns, where a company of soldiers could be lodged, and where perhaps ten beds are made up. The town is well worth resting in, and if the traveller is there on a church *fête* day he will see

From a drawing]   WARTENBERG.   *[by Walter Crane.*

some interesting sights and quaint costumes, and the drive onwards to Turnau is full of beauty, and change, and interest.

But before visiting these we must take a run by rail away to the north to embrace an active commercial centre, and to visit the historic town of Friedland, that lies so near the Saxon frontier.

Friedland lies to the extreme north of the Kingdom of Bohemia, and the line to it from Turnau passes through a very lovely country. After leaving Reichenberg the line runs between wooded hills and green valleys with well-tilled plateaus and prosperous-looking villages. Then come stretches of wild forest and high hills, with frequent tunnels ; and on arriving at Friedland the drive into it from the station is suggestive of much of interest. It is a clean, pleasant little town, rarely troubled with tourists; an Englishman is a curiosity. Its central square is surrounded with pointed and rounded gabled houses, reminding one of Bruges, in the middle of which stands the square Brunnen and high column, with the women around it; and above this rises the tower of the Town Hall, and above all, high on its rocky peak, looms up the dominating castle.

Friedland reminds one somewhat of little Dunster, the hunting town in Devonshire. The walk up to the castle is between hedgerows that again call up Devonshire to the mind. The round tower over the arch gateway, the high roofs and gables and pinnacles, and beyond the old part and red triple domed tower, remind one of Scotland and the châteaux on the Loire. The moat is in disorder, but the drawbridge is in perfect order, the chains ready to swing it up, should a hostile entrance be threatened. Over the entrance are coats of arms, the lower one ostrich feathers with eagles, three helms and arrows.

From a drawing]   DEWIN CASTLE.   *[by Walter Cross.*

After passing beneath a square tower with a pointed arch, there opens up a most charming peep beyond of another pointed arch, with portcullis ready to fall. Around the first great tower are numerous stags' heads, and then we enter into a little courtyard, and as we approach the second arch the inner court opens up scenically, and around it are towers and gables, oriels and dormer windows, towers square, and round, and octagonal. The work is of various ages, new and old, speaking emphatically of history. A little balcony overhangs one part. One can easily picture it filled with dames waving a welcome to incoming knights.

Over the lower central tower door are the coloured modern arms of Clam-Gallas, and above these the old plaque with the bronze older arms. Up through this gate we pass, and yet ahead is another arch, and now we can see the regular columns of basalt supporting the great central building and tower. The whole castle has been built *down* in successive ages round this peaked basalt cone of pillars; its earliest part being perched on the cone peak. Up through this arch we go on in wonderment to the central court; over the round tower is the date 1014. This was the kernel of this great castle, a round watch-tower; and from this kernel has grown this mighty interesting building. In 1248, Berka von Duba built the part round this tower, the date is on the building, and on the other side is a little arcade. A part of the castle was burnt in 1500. For nearly three hundred years it was in the possession of the Bibersteins, then it passed into the hands of the Lords of Radern, and in 1622 Albert of Wallenstein bought it for 150,000 florins, and after his death it was presented by the Emperor Ferdinand II. to Count Mathias Gallas, whose family intermarried with the Clams; and in the hands of the family of Clam-Gallas it still remains. The Gallas family also inter-married with the mighty race of the Rosenbergs, so that they possessed great influence.

[*From a drawing*]   BÖHMISCH AICHA.   [*by Walter Crane.*]

In a work of this description no attempt will be made to give a consecutive history of Bohemia and her people; but these old castles present to us pictures of mediæval life, and as we visit other parts of this mountain-locked land we shall see spots that recall her earlier history, when Poland's king was Bohemia's ruler, or when Bohemia's overlord commanded a race that still worshipped the old gods and sacrificed on the mountain-side or in forest's depths. Tradition of these days still exist, and super-stition still supports strange heathen customs, for as late even as the fifteenth century Bohemia had heathen for her neighbours on north and

east, and in the very districts where legend and superstition still cling to
the minds of the inhabitants will be found an active busy life, well abreast
with all the energy and intellectual activity of to-day.

The fact that Bohemia still preserves much of her mediæval ideas and
life, while living a vigorous modern existence, is indicated by the sight
in this beautiful old courtyard of a fine iron lamp held out from the wall
by a hand, showing the artistic taste of the present owners of the castle.
This arrests the attention as we ring the bell, and when the door opens we
enter a little Romanesque hall hung with portraits, in which is a model of
the old buildings of the castle. The interior of the castle is as interesting
as the exterior, and as full of interesting objects as a museum. One
portrait not to be overlooked is the authentic one of the great Wallenstein,
Duke of Friedland, painted in 1626. A thin face, massive, high, square
forehead, something sad and stern, and with a bit of a sneer in the expression ;
a little moustache and pointed beard of reddish hair ; this was painted when
he was forty-three years of age. The portrait of Ceni,· his astrologer, is of
interest, and Ceni's writing is curiously like Charles Pebody's, the late
editor of the *Yorkshire Post.* There is a good plan of Friedland in 1660 ;
the town then had double walls and round watch towers. The Square just
as it now is. There is also a collection of articles belonging to Wallenstein,
and a head of Moreau, the young French general who was quartered here
at the Battle of Dresden.

As we pass on through these halls and corridors the interest increases,
until at length we reach the great central tower, the castle's germ, and here
at the summit of all these buildings, three great iron doors are swung back,
and in through walls nearly twelve feet thick is the awful dungeon of the
castle, in the living rock, the basalt kernel. Prisoners here were thrust not
down into the *oubliette,* but taken to the summit of the castle, and yet
thrust into the silent rock, to where no sound of maiden's lute or mad
revelry could pierce. To make things doubly sure, the heavy triple door is
of iron plates bound over with bands of iron. The old room in this tower
is like the Romersaal at Frankfort, and contains a collection of war trophies
and weapons, lances, and axes, and clubs, and an executioner's axe ; and,
to be well noted, the famous Hussite flails and morning stars. A terrible
weapon was this flail, with a long staff, at the end of which was a shorter
staff slung on with a chain, this being bound with iron and with spikes
upon it. The morning stars are long staves with an iron ball at the end,
with spikes all over, and a long spike at the end ; both fearful weapons for
hand combat.

But Friedland Castle is holding us too long, and yet, with that of
Krumau in South Bohemia, it is one of those that for nearly a thousand
years has had a living existence, and still through its indwellers plays a
part in the history of the country. Around its towered heights, down in

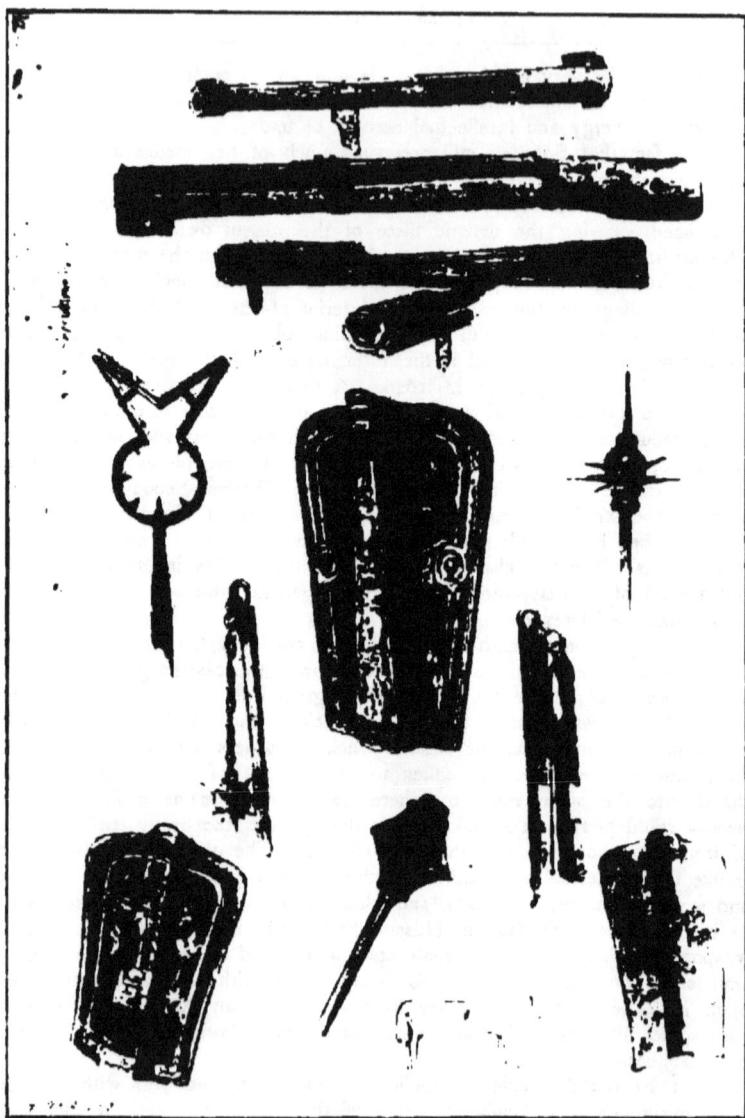

the town beneath, reigns a busy commercial life, one takes, as it were, a plunge from historic heights, from mediæval life in castle halls, to every-day commercial activity. Lords and serving men change to employer and employed. All around the castle are factories, and through the castle park in early morn and late eve go the busy earnest workers, and the theme of foreign competition can well be studied here, for the hours of labour are long, and the pay small. Men at the cloth factories earn four to five gulden a week, say eight shillings and sixpence. Girls but two to three gulden, say six francs or five shillings; and yet as these girls cross over the little bridges in the park, they are far more neatly dressed than our factory hands, and the men also look neat, well shod, and by no means of a starved expression; their working hours are twelve per day. In the fields the wages are still less, men earning two to three gulden, and women one-and-a-half to two gulden. As a labourer exclaimed, to whom we chatted: 'Anyone who gets four or five gulden here is well off.'

Anyone who would understand the industry of the Bohemian must know these figures, and bear them in mind as he travels through the minutely-tilled land, teeming with factories sending their work throughout the world. Friedland is a German-speaking district, and the children respond to your questions in German. One looks up from the whirr of machinery and clack of mills, and there above in lordly pride rises the old tower that for centuries has dominated the town, its triple red dome glowing in the sunlight; and the scene is so picturesque it is with difficulty one quits it to look into the church with its interesting monuments, and statues in bronze, and marble, and granite.

Living here is remarkably cheap, breakfast and dinner costing but eighteen-pence. It should be remembered that at all these inns meals should at once be paid for, only the rooms go on the bill. Somewhat astonished at the marvellous interest of both town and castle, we called for the visitors' book, and went back for three years, but no English name was to be found. When we left to go to the station we found a well turned-out carriage and pair waiting to drive us there, with two men on the box, coachman in silver buttons and cockade. We objected to this extravagance, asking what was the cost. 'It is on the bill,' was the answer. As it had not been noticed we did not venture to look at the bill until in the train, and then we saw the charge was twenty kreutzers, or threepence halfpenny.

At Friedland, Peaceland—how suggestive the name seemed! for its busy industrious life and quiet parks and walks are on the extreme border of Bohemia we must retrace our steps to Reichenberg. As we draw near to this manufacturing town, the valleys have great factories in them, looking not unsightly, they are so tiny amid the great hills; the green fields have lines of cloth lying along them, dyeing and drying. The whole country looks bright and prosperous, and as we halt at Reichenberg we count forty-three factory chimneys in sight. Cloth weaving commenced in this town late in the sixteenth century, and has developed into a great industry. But although Reichenberg dates back to early in the fourteenth century—the Bibersteins and Wallensteins were its overlords—there is little of antiquity left to occupy us, and we soon hastened away from the clack of the loom and drove on to Gablonz, the great centre of the glass trade of Bohemia.

Gablonz lies close up under the Giant Mountains, being itself some 1500 feet above sea-level; entirely a new town, only receiving the name of town in this century, and not yet connected with the railway, yet sending its manufactures over all the world. Here the wholly modern life of Bohemia may be studied, no embattled castle throwing thought back into past days. Hard, strenuous, intelligent labour, with quick changes from intense work to careless gaiety and enjoyment. A walk up to the Schutzenhaus, or rifle range, gives a good view of Gablonz and its encircling mountains. The whole valley filled with houses, a gentle sound of labour comes up, but no roar: free pure air and sky, and green fields and forests around. Much of the work is done in the homes of the workers, and as we halted, and were pointed out the various points of interest, there came up to us the weird sad harmonious strains of a funeral march, and we saw wending along the hillside the train of mourners in many colours, save the near relatives, for in Bohemia, as in Ireland, all join in at a funeral.

In Gablonz may be studied not only the general and home industries of Bohemia, but the great reason of Austria's seizing so much of the world's commerce, and becoming of late years so fierce and dangerous a competitor to England—her most excellent technical schools. Whatever trade a district embraces, a good technical school is established to teach that trade, how to develop and improve it: the technical school here is most well ordered. At the invitation of a manufacturer, we joined him in a drive into some distant villages to visit his outlying work-people who work in their own homes. The villages visited were those of Neudorf and Wiesenthal and Morgenstein, this latter little town being in the Great Mountain district; and the tour of these mountains might be commenced here. Full of busy life was every home; the cottages often being of two rooms only, and with windows all closed against the sharp mountain air. The rooms over-heated, and serving as workshops, living-rooms, and bed-rooms, and yet smart and clean. The beds, with their large pink *duvet*, or down quilts, neatly covered over with lace-like coverings, and the few cooking utensils bright and clean. Little stags' heads decorated the walls, with bright common pictures. Here we saw them making women's glass dress ornaments and glass trinkets; and even in these small villages were little theatres and the inevitable dancing-rooms.

It was with a sense of regret, a feeling often experienced in quitting our quarters in Bohemia, that we left these hospitable mountain valleys, and took the ordinary *Stellwagen* into Reichenau, where at a little hut station on a high plateau of rock, field, and forest, we awaited the train that took us back again into Turnau. The town of Turnau has been much modernised. It is of respectable antiquity, a Dominican monastery having been founded here in the thirteenth century; but it has suffered terribly from war, even in 1866 having to pay Prussia dearly for her conquering army.

The central square is varied with its churches, the one pinnacled, the other with dome and cross, its Jacobean houses, and barracks, and soldiers on guard. In the centre the Brunnen, with tall white pillars, gilt capitols and figure of Christ, and the group seated around it of marketers in all colours, with their booths and covered carts, and produce, forming a *tout ensemble* of picturesque effect. Perhaps halting, half lounging, is a group of Bohemian or Moravian tramps. The former with dark Eastern faces, long hair, and very dirty; a high Tyrolean type of hat, and big jack-boots, and short postillion-like jackets, with a leather sabretache-like bag slung over the shoulder, covered with bright brass plaques. The Moravians wear long white coats with black embroidery, baggy white leather breeches with black patterns worked

AN OLD HOUSE IN TURNAU : DATE 1816.
(From a Drawing by Walter Crane.)

on them, jack-boots, and slouched hats. They come up into the glass districts of Bohemia as pedlars; their chief is more gaily dressed than the others, and he does the buying. They then work their way, selling as they go, even down into Hungary, where railways do not bring competition. To meet some of these groups on a country road suggests brigands, and thoughts of being borne off into some of the mountain recesses and being held for rich ransom; but they are only peaceful and reliable traders, say the Bohemian manufacturers, and their costumes help to bring back the past in this land, so full of antiquity, yet living.

The technical school at Turnau is well worth a careful visit, and so are the precious stone establishments ; for, strange as it may seem, Turnau boasts of being, and is, a great centre for jewels. The expense of the technical schools is divided between the town and the State ; the town giving building and fire, the State officials, materials and models. The education is free, and poor lads are even assisted with from five to ten guldens a month if they are talented, and in this town of only 6000 inhabitants, the complete course of technical and practical teaching is thorough and more effective, for it goes on from theory to actual work, than our South Kensington method ; and this teaching is decentralised, within reach of every one in his own district. In one jewel-finishing and manufacturing establishment, where they were fabricating turquoise in round slabs, we were left alone in a room full of trays of thousands of jewels of amethyst and rubies, onyx and emeralds, and above all garnets, for Turnau is a great garnet district, and some very beautiful parures are produced here in the cottage workshops.

From a drawing)   ROCKS AT GROS SKAL.   *[by Walter Crane.*

Among the chief places to be visited around Turnau are the Klein Skal and the Gros or Great Skal. On the principle that the greater includes the less, we shall describe only the strange sights which embrace the castles and rock towers of Gros Skal and Waldstein. Soon after leaving the carriage we dived into the forest between the great pine masts ; and soon also between great isolated pillars of sandstone, rising up suddenly from the brown forest flooring, and towering in isolated grandeur to the height of 300 feet. These Titanic pillars soon grew thicker ; at one spot was a grotto scooped out and dedicated to St. Prokop : generally in these forest and rock solitudes there is a praying-place. The strange awe and

From a water-colour drawing] KLEIN SKAL *[by Walter Crane*

mystery of the forest depths, and of these rock recesses are so impressive in their weird mystery, that instinctively a tremor seizes on one, and thoughts of the supernatural and of evil spirits take possession of the mind. Hence the peasants have turned them into praying-places to the God who can alone deliver from evil. In one place, as we climbed upwards, we were amidst a hundred to a hundred-and-twenty of these sandstone pillars, all grotesquely shaped, worn and scratched.

At one spot a most singular sight was seen. We halted and looked straight up between the pillars and the pines, and high up as it were in the sky, and glittering against the deep blue of heaven, were the little towers of a castle, at least 600 feet above us, and almost perpendicularly so. In one narrow gorge the winter snow still lay, and the air was icily cold. In another the great wall of rocks looked like great ogres' heads, with eyes and twisted mouths, then came a narrow pass called the Mouse's Hole, with steps giving just room for one man to pass up at a time. Slits in the rock seemed to give a chance of getting up without passing through the Mouse's Hole, but all these slits were illusive, and traps to those who ventured into them. Then came a circular rocky space as an open justice hall, above which were a few steps, and, hey presto ! the scene changes from awful forest and rock solitude to an open space, with a bridge leading across to a feudal castle, and an inn with carriages and horses, and entertainment for man and beast. Marvellous and astonishing are these sudden transformations, like the Bohemian character and the Bohemian music, from intense pathos to wild joy, from a funeral to a dance.

The castle courtyard and inn buildings hid all view, but passing through the inn we found lunch awaiting us, actually on the summit of one of the great rock piers, from the base of which we had caught the glimpse of this then aerial appearing castle, and from this giddy perch a strange but most lovely view circled round us. High above the pine tops, far away, rose up the strange twin towers of Trosky. Sheer down into the valley we could look amidst the rock pillars, and then away over valleys and fields and forests to a distant range of mountains.

This picture illustrates excellently the difficulty a foreign foe would have in attacking these mountain nests and recesses. Even in 805, Charlemagne proved that to conquer Bohemia was no light task. He sent against it three great armies from south, east, and north. The Bohemians were surprised, and fell back to their mountains ; the armies of Charlemagne met on the plains near Saaz and Leitmeritz, but the guerilla mountain warfare defeated them, and they left Bohemia without compelling its chiefs to submit or pay tribute, though for forty days they devasted the plains. And yet a thousand years later in 1866, the Prussians marched through this district to Königgrätz, and in this mountain top of Gros Skal, in the little forest cemetery amid rock-hewn tombs, lies buried a lieutenant who fell at Jicin in that year.

A pleasant pathway leads through and over the rock town to the Castle of Waldstein. The local legends that are told of these castles and of the rock recesses are well worth studying, and they help one to understand the passionate fierce life that has surged around these castle walls in old days, and of the dread of the peasant as he passed beneath, lest he should hear the shrieks of some tortured victim or oppressed maiden. And one little wonders at the belief in the supernatural, as we pass on amid the white keeps and towers, bastions and pillars of the natural rock towns. The rocks are of a sandstone and chalk formation, and thus easily water-worn and shaped grotesquely. One great rock was as a giant's sarcophagus, at another spot thirty to forty great pillars rise up. On another white rock a gigantic hand had been l a i d flat, and scorched the mark of palms, fingers, and thumbs upon it. Of course the Devil's hand. Other rocks were toned with a delicate grey l i c h e n, and others with the brilliant sulphur, again the Devil's handy-work.

(From a drawing by Walter Crane.)

At length we emerge from this wild primeval maze, and enter a plateau where cultivated fields take the place of rocks and pines, and ere long an open space faces the Renaissance bridge with statues of saints upon it, leading into the ruins of the Castle of Waldstein, or Waldenstein, from whence that family take their name. Waldstein, like Gros Skal, is perched nest-like upon pillars of rock; but a level plateau on one side affords space for a cottage or two and gardens; and near here are traces of earthworks that edge the forest. Crossing the bridge, a little chapel of modern date is seen, and passing round this a gate is opened by the keeper, and suddenly is seen an embattled platform built up some seventy feet from the forest below. The old ruin, which is reached as usual by a narrow path between the solid rock, has been scooped out into chambers and port-holes, pierced through it to command the entrance. The castle was built in the twelfth century, and many are the interesting notes of the Lords of Waldstein in Bohemian history. In 1409, a certain Wok or Woksa of Waldstein was a favourite of King Wenzel, and he it was who in 1412, when Hus was preaching continually in the Bethlehem Chapel at Prague, with the queen as a devout

listener, ordered and carried out a similar scene to that witnessed at Wittenberg a century later. He arranged a procession that passed before the archbishop's house in the Kleinseite, then crossed over the famous Carls bridge, and through the old town to the Graben or moat of the new town, and here a great pyre had been built, on which the Pope's bulls were laid, and amidst the jubilations of the surrounding multitude the whole was set in flames, defying the papal power: and though the king, rather than break wholly with Rome, forbade his nobles to commit any open excesses against the Pope, yet Woksa of Waldstein went unpunished and remained his favourite, and Hus still had the queen as a listener to his preaching. Woksa had the honour a little later on of being com-

(From a drawing by Walter Crane.)

manded to appear before the Romish Curia with others, as the notorious supporter of heretics.

But to dwell upon all the incidents connected with Waldstein in Bohemian history is impossible, as we wander amidst its ruins and climb up to its highest battlements and look out over the wild expanse of country its towers commanded, some deeper insight into the turbulent life of the great period of Bohemia's history can be gained from its dungeons and towers and ruined halls.

THE 'DOVE' HEAD-DRESS OF A BOHEMIAN MAIDEN.

CHAPTER IV.

JICIN AND ITS SURROUNDINGS.

IN driving away from Turnau onwards towards Königgrätz, a very enjoyable day may be arranged, halting for the night at Jicin, where the railway can be used, if the traveller is tired of the slower method of travelling behind a couple of good horses. The twin castle peaks that from all heights have been calling and tempting us to climb them, form the first halting stage. Old defiant Trosky, that has reared its twin towers on its sister peaks for so many centuries, is from its situation one of the most remarkable sights in this castle-peaked land. From Trosky we drove through forest and scattered villages, until we reached another ruined castle. So thickly are these ruined castles scattered in this district, that it became a standing joke in the morning ere we started on our drives, to ask how many castles we were to 'do' in the day. And yet so deftly are they ofttimes hidden in the mountain recesses, that travellers pass amidst them and know nothing of them. A notable instance of this was the case of Mrs.

Joseph Pennell, the American, who in her ride from Berlin to Buda-Pesth piteously says of this very district between Aussig on the Elbe and Prague: 'What is the use of an old country if it has no old stuff to show for its years?' and again, after riding from Prague to Carlsbad, she exclaims: 'After Carlsbad we came to the one and only real castle we saw in Bohemia.' Nothing old! and yet this American lady was in sight of, had she only known it, and might have visited, at least fifty mediæval castles in ruins or still inhabited!

We entered Kost in torrents of rain, but the advantage of driving

From a drawing)   KOST CASTLE.   (by Walter Crane.

through these districts is that the carriages can quickly be closed; luckily so, for the rain descends in sheets, and instantaneously, in these mountain districts. We entered the little inn, its one room forming workshop, kitchen, bed-, drawing-room, and guest-chamber. From the inn windows we had a good view of the castle, standing most picturesquely amidst strange pointed yellow rocks, and above a little lake. Its walls were embattled, and the great square tower or keep was of a curious shape, being an irregular square, so that from one view all four corners can be seen at once. There is a similarly shaped tower at Beaucaire in France, on the Rhone, opposite Tarascon. A lesser tower was round. The castle court is now a farmyard, but interesting bits of its former greatness are left. On the castle wall is a

E 2

boar's head and some good scroll work, and in the little chapel some good
early glass; one bit depicting knight and Virgin in good preservation.

From this pretty spot we drove on again through a rich cultivated
district of orchards, and large farms buried in fruit-blossom, to the town of
Sobotka.   The great square at Sobotka preserves some of the old timber
houses, with galleries supported on timber piers, the type of house still seen

SADOWA.

in the villages, but fast disappearing.   It is an old-world town, the church
is of some interest, one quaint rude monument of a knight in armour of
1599 attracted our attention; but a long drive on to Jicin still awaiting
us, we soon harnessed our horses, and drove on across the battle plain
of Jicin.

Jicin is another town that makes an excellent centre for drives and
excursions.   Very numerous are the ruined castles around it, and singular
but gigantic freaks of Nature as the Prachov rock-town.   The town itself is

of somewhat later date than many of these Bohemian towns, but it was raised to the rank of town in 1302, so it is of respectable age. Its importance dates from Wallenstein, who built a famous castle here. Wallenstein also commenced the Dechanel church of St. Jacob in the style of the church of St. Jago of Campostello, but his murder arrested this work, and it was finished by his successor in 1655.

The place of widest interest in the neighbourhood of Jicin is Königgrätz, standing on a broad tableland like the great battle-plains of Leipzig and

From a drawing]   A MARKET IN KÖNIGGRATZ.   *[by H. Whatley.*

Waterloo, with only rising uplands and wooded mounds here and there to block the wide expanse of view. In the town itself but little is seen to recall the sad day of July 3, 1866, when near by, on the Jicin road, some 50,000 men were done to death in battle. It was about an hour's walk from Königgrätz that the culminating battle took place that closed the Seven Weeks' War. The headquarters of the Prussian Army were at Sadowa, hence the naming of the battle from this place by the victors. The most terrible part of the fighting occurred in and around the small forest called Wobora, that for five hours was attacked, and defended by the Prussians to keep open communication with the expected army of the Crown

Prince, 'Our Fritz,' who came up just as the Austrians, after fearful sacrifice, had carried the wood. It is saddening work to walk over these battlefields, and to think of the misery of wives and children, mothers and fathers, waiting in their homes for death news, and of the awful sufferings of men and animals lying writhing in agonies on the battle-plain, and it is with relief we turn back into the town, and in early morning wander round the Ring, amid the marketers and the peaceful workers in homely life.

Here the scene is not so picturesque as in many of the southern towns, where the costume adds brilliancy to the operatic grouping of the peasants. The Great Ring at Königgrätz is an oblong, rather than a square, and leads into what is known as the Kleine, or Little Ring. In its centre stands a high column with a statue of the Madonna, with figures round its base. In the upper corner stands the brick Gothic Cathedral, reminding one of the brick architecture of Lubeck somewhat, and by its side, adjoining the St. Clemence Chapel, towers up the high White Tower, where perchance may be seen in its upper balcony the watchman and his wife, now and then calling down to a passing friend a salutation from their lonely up-post. At one side of the square are the domed towers of the Maria Church, with some trees before its doors, and on the north (opposite) side the houses are arcaded.

Perchance the stone balls now lying by the Prague gate may date from the time when Königgrätz, in company with Prague and Tabor, were the hottest enemies of Kaiser Sigmund. In 1436, a priest (Ambrosius) led the Hussites here most energetically, called a knight of Raudnitz with armed men to his aid, and openly declared the town to be against the Kaiser. Forces from all sides were sent against it, and surrounded it, causing a famine; but the Raudnitz knight, named Monch, took advantage of a dark night, and sallied out, stormed their waggons, burnt their huts, and slew their leader as he slept, says one chronicler. Another of the enemy's foremost men had to fly to the Kuneticer Castle, that we had seen on the height near Pardubic. A would-be mediator with the Emperor, who came to Königgrutz, was thrown into a dungeon as an answer. But in the following year the Kaiser's party began to gain power; Monch himself seems to have bid for the Emperor's favour at Prague, and returning to Königgrätz, roused the folk against Ambrosius. Out into the Ring came this priest with the Host uplifted, but his enemies were too many for him, and he fled to the walls; but to fall from them, breaking his arms and legs, and thus he was taken prisoner. The people of Königgrätz appointed new councillors, and sent to the Kaiser, saying they would be obedient to his rule; but with the added independent statement, that for a time no new councillors were to be placed over them, and they were not to be asked for any money, nor be required to build any monasteries. Which free and outspoken terms the Kaiser thought it advisable to accept.

This sketch of incidents of the years 1436 and 1437 well illustrates

From a drawing]   [by H. Whalley.

ROCK TOWN AT PRACHOWER FELSEN,' CASTLE TROSKY IN THE DISTANCE.

the life of this turbulent period, and also the sturdy self-assertion of the people, a quality they still possess.

To illustrate the district around Jicin fully would occupy far more space than we can give; but the traveller who finds himself in comfortable quarters at the Stadt Hamburg Hotel, just outside the great high tower and gate known as the Waldicer Thor, can well find entertainment in excursions around the town for a week. Hard by is the high hill upon which stands all that is left of the once powerful Castle of Welis, where up to the year 1500 the famous 'Compact' was guarded as a most precious document. Not far from this castle is the village of Kbelince, one of those peaceful sad scenes that tell of war and bloodshed. There is here a little cemetery in which were buried some of those who fell in the battles around Jicin in 1866. It is but a tiny graveyard, with pyramids and columns, and shrubs and trees and flowers in good order. One monument was erected by the 'sorrowing mother and wife.' A curious but symbolic tomb was that of a pile of stones, from out of which a snake was creeping and curling. Friend and foe are buried here, Prussian, Saxon, and Austrian; and as we looked round on the spring promising landscape, so lovely and so peaceful, and then at this roadside cemetery, with isolated monuments here and there in the fields and roadside all around, 'What an accursed thing war is!' came involuntarily to our lips.

From Jicin may be explored the labyrinths and recesses of the picturesque Prachower Felsen, or Rock Town. To enter these rock towns without a guide is useless. Generally a peasant in the near village can be persuaded to join the stranger, but without a guide one is quickly lost amid the mazes of the rock pillars. A Professor of Jicin kindly acted as our cicerone, and on reaching what is called the first Kanape, we had a magnificent view of the gigantic rock piers and towers, especially one mighty mass called the Rabenfelsen. A little to the right of this rose Trosky, the ruin that asserts itself and will be seen wherever one stands in its neighbourhood. Below, some two or three hundred feet, amidst pines and fresh foliaged trees, were the roots of three great rock pillars; and in amongst the giant columns we passed, amid fir-trees and peeps of wonderful rock masses, until we came out upon the summit of one great pier called Trostein, where were the ashes of an annual witches' fire, that the peasants had burnt amidst this weird scene at midnight of April 30.

Once more from this point of view we were led on to yet another sudden change of view; now we looked down into the Rundgang, or Arena, where it was said in the days of persecution the Bohemian Brotherhood held their secret meetings for prayer; and from this point a narrow steep descent between great walls of rock led us down the Kaisergang, or Emperors' Passage, a silent solemn pass amid the piers of rock : only from the upper open air came the hum of insect life and twitter and chirp of birds. Here at one point the rock was worn into the semblance of a great mouth with a tongue lolling out, and this was called the Devil's Mouth. Far down in the depths we halted, at a spot where was indeed a most wonderful retrospect, looking back to the end of the Kaisergang. Great masses of rock as enormous wall towers, with strange grotesque formations, were all around us, and as we were deep in the depths of these passes, heavy clouds swept over the blue sky and deepened the gloom and increased the weird solemnity of the scene.

At the extreme end of this labyrinth of rocks is a rock castle, where in bygone times some robber lord had scooped out a refuge for himself, somewhat after the manner of Mickisch at Burgstein; and here a pre-historic burying-place has also been discovered. In some places the rocks are honeycombed with deep cells. We went on through the deep arena, and up to the second Kanape, from whence some quaint rocks could be seen, one of the Madonna and Child; another as of a frog, another as a bishop with his mitre; and from this point a narrow path led up to a spot where a summer-house was erected with some steps that led up to a look-out over all the district. The name of this spot was Svincice (pronounced Swincheatsay), and very much surprised were our Bohemian friends, that by means of this phonetic spelling we were enabled to pronounce its name fairly accurately, for Cech pronunciation is very difficult to a foreigner. Here all the points that can be discerned from this look-out are marked on the encircling parapet, and the view is very varied and very beautiful. When we quitted it we dived once more into the clefts of the rocks to what is called the Great Gate, where a ponderous mass of rock has fallen over, leaving a narrow pass under it; near it a rock is formed into a perfect giant mushroom, and on the side of one of the rocks are incised curious marks, that none yet have explained: some say treasure is buried here, others that these were marks of the Bohemian Brethren.

Our exit from these rocks was made from another pass to that by which we entered; thus we used the only two entrances to the rocks, and as we emerged above the lovely village of Locher, all nestled amid fruit-trees, an old woman dressed in red blue and yellow was ascending the hill with the inevitable load upon her back, the whole forming a fascinating picture of peace and beauty.

As we sat chatting over our busy days amidst these strange and historic scenes, we were reminded that Jicin was 'at present' the only town that had a monument to Hus, and a Hus Street. And we were told also of two other famous men connected with Jicin, both of whom sought a refuge in England. The one Commenius, and the other Wenzel Hollar, the engraver, who became a favourite at the court of Charles I.

Jicin is a good point of departure for the Giant Mountain district of Bohemia. The trains move along very gently, one can sometimes keep

From a drawing]   ROCK TOWN AT ADERSBACH.   [by H. Whatley.

pace afoot with them ; and to reach Trautenau, or Hohenelbe, the round to Alt-Paka is so wide that time even may be saved by driving pleasantly to this junction.

The town of Trautenau has not so much of mediæval or archæological interest as many other towns in Bohemia, but it was one of the first points of attack of one line of the Prussian advance in 1866 ; and the heights behind the town, now laid out as a people's park, bear awful evidence of the fighting. All up the hill are scattered crosses and monuments, and at the top is an old strongly-built chapel, its walls still dotted with bullets that rained here thickly on June 27th, 1866 ; and around this St. John's chapel are lines of crosses and monuments to the dead who were slain on that day. Especially one to Lieutenant Budenbruch, who found a pass up the height and stormed it with a company of East Prussians who had never before seen a hill, and in his victory was killed.

The monument to the Austrian Field-Marshal Gablenz, commanding on this day (a day of victory to the Austrians), is situated on a neighbouring height called the Gablenzhohe, and from this spot the whole district round Trautenau can be viewed. The deep valleys all filled; with factories, yet not so thickly as to look unsightly, or to poison the pure air of the mountain ranges that tower above them.

The lonely little house, as seen from here, on the summit of the Schneekoppe, is clearly, visible ; and it is from Trautenau that the climb can be made to this highest point of the Giant Mountains. One route; is by Johannisbad and through the Dunkle Thal (Dark Valley), whence a two and a half hours' walk will take the climber to the summit ; or another way is to go to Hohenelbe, and from there make the still easier ascent. The spring is too early to make this climb with pleasure ; in early summer or in September are the best seasons. We have seen in May from Trautenau the whole Schneekoppe free from snow, tempting one to the ascent, and the next morning the whole line of hills pure and glistening with deep fresh snow, telling of what we should have experienced had the ascent been attempted.

But there is an excursion from Trautenau that can be made with advantage in springtime, the drive to the strange rock towns of Adersbach and Weckelsdorf. We had already visited many of the rock towns of Northern Bohemia, but were hardly prepared for the immensity and grotesque weirdness of the rock labyrinth of Adersbach.

The road from Adersbach to Weckelsdorf reminds one much of the English Wye ; the rounding sweeps of the river with the precipitous high rocks, though here the rocks are more mighty, and the pines give a sombreness to the scenery, which is relieved however by the birch and flowering fruit-trees. But this entrance to the gorge hardly prepares one for the Titanic great-ness of Nature's architecture within the labyrinths. Here, as at Adersbach, Nature has curiously copied man's representations. Johan of Nepomuc, wearing his biretta, stands high up amid towering columns and castle keeps, three hundred feet in height. Not far from him sits the 'Jager,' resting from the chase with leg outstretched; here and there from the summit of the piers peep over a partridge, or a turtle, or an owl, most perfect in shape. In what is called the market-place the rocks are formed as great cloth rolls lying on one another, and in the dom or cathedral place beyond, the mighty wall of rock is worked into a great blind Romanesque arch, with good mouldings; and just beyond this the crypt is entered of this Nature's cathedral.

In spite of our being the 'swallows' that told of the summer, and that we were alone with our guide, as we entered the Cathedral an organ commenced playing; at first we thought detracting from the intense solemnity and grandeur of the rock architecture, but as the rock roofs threw back with deep toned reverberations the Austrian national hymn of Haydn, we felt thankful for this addition to our pleasure.

Of all these rock towns Weckelsdorf is the most terrific and mighty; but Adersbach has peculiar charms and more artistic points, and the lesser rock towns of Prachow, and Gros Skal, and Klein Skal, have each their peculiar beauties and especial charms. We were fortunate to have seen them exactly reversed to the above order, and in this order of Klein Skal first we should recommend travellers to visit them.

From a drawing]   GABLENZ HEIGHT.   *[by N. Whatley.*

CHAPTER V.

KUTTENBERG AND ITS ASSOCIATIONS.

THE powerfully descriptive chapters in Palacky's [1] most admirable history of Bohemia, of the events that centred around the town of Kuttenberg, or Kutna Hora, to give it the Cech spelling, first led us to visit that town. But his descriptions, exciting as they are and full of graphic power, did not prepare us for all the pleasure we had from our visit. We entered the town late on a hot evening in May, and were soon housed in a most comfortable old-world inn ; and finding the population nearly wholly Cech, we produced our letters of introduction from Count Thun and others, and begged the landlord to get some German-speaking gentleman who could give us some information about the town and its history. The result was curious.

We waited until dark came, but no kindly guide made his appearance ; our host, in fair German, said he had sent twice for someone, but he had not come ; so we made our first acquaintance the beautiful St. Barbara's church alone with an outside glimpse ; and after seeing some other parts of the town returned to supper. What we had seen convinced us there was

[1] Pronounced 'Palatzky.'

very much of historical interest still left in the town, and again we begged
for some cicerone, but no one came.

In the morning we expressed our surprise that no professor, or school-
master, or cleric, as in other towns, had offered us some information.

THE BARRACK; KUTTENBERG.

'Well,' said the landlord, 'I have sent two or three times to the editor
of the paper here, who knows well the history of our town, and I can't
understand why he does not come; I will send again.'

A messenger was despatched, and in a quarter of an hour a gentleman, wearing a straw hat, arrived. He looked us up and down, and then raising his hat, said in German—

'Gentlemen, I must apologise. I was told that four Englishmen had come to see the town, and wanted my guidance. We never had any English-men here, and never expected to have any, and I thought our club that meets here was playing a joke on me.'

We thanked him for his courtesy in coming now, and we afterwards had to thank this M. Gustav Touzil, editor of the local newspaper, for a great deal of help. He did his utmost to tell us all he could, and when he could not be with us him-self, he got some good neighbour to join us, and he hailed our advent in his Cech paper with an article headed 'Strange guests.'

The crowning beauty of Kuttenberg is the very remark-able church, or rather fragment of a church, dedicated to St. Bar-bara. It is really only the choir of a great cathedral, but

CHURCH OF ST. JACOBI, KUTTENBERG.

this choir is so great in its proportions, that it is nearly as large as some of our English cathedrals. The approach to it is along a terrace with a barrack on one hand, and groups of Renaissance figures along the parapet on the other. The barrack was formerly a Jesuit College, and most of the Renais-sance work in Kuttenberg is due to Jesuit influence. The groups of statues under the trees that overshadow them are picturesque, and remind one of the famous Carls Bridge at Prague; one of the best figures is that of St. Wenzel, clinging to the great knocker of the church for sanctuary, as his brother's dagger pierces him.

As the east end of the church is approached, all its beauty breaks magnificently upon one. It is a very extraordinary piece of work, with double flying buttress, with rounded arches and crochetted carvings both above and below. The numberless pinnacles are most richly ornamented, and the mouldings of the windows, though somewhat thin, are very delicate in design and most varied. The intricacies of the architecture are rich, and the general design is effective. If the view of the church from this end is very charming, so also is the extent of the surrounding country ; for the church is perched high up on a rocky hill-side, and from its east and south sides commands a wide expanse of view. To the left rises up the tall tower of St. Jacobi, dominating the town, that is some 150 feet from the plain below. Peasants in most brilliant colours are walking along a road at the foot of a wall of grey rocks. On a lower level is the thin sharp tower of St. Marie's Himmelfahrt, and above the wall of rock, on a green mound, stands a mine wheel, that reminds one that Kuttenberg was once the purse of Bohemia, and supplied the silver from its mines for the coinage.

OLD STALLS IN THE CHURCH OF ST. JACOBI.

The interior of this magnificent church fragment is as interesting as the exterior. One entrance to it was by means of a covered passage on arches from the Jesuit College. This piece of Jacobean arching has just been cleared away, which is a pity, as it speaks of an epoch in its history, although of a type of architecture so different from the main building. Other marvels of this architectural date are the florid ugly skull and cross-bones work at the south porch. The north is still in the Pointed style. This later work has sometimes been introduced to deface Hussite work, especially the hated sign of the Chalice. The triforium gallery is of fine open work, and in the *ambulatoire* behind the choir is a curious use of the flamboyant type of architecture.

In the west end of the church are preserved some fine Renaissance Jacobean stalls and confessionals, and before them is an altar in front of the sacristy. One of the pillars here is found to be of wood, and half-way up it is a peep-hole, whence a spy from the Jesuits could watch confessor and confessed. On the west wall over the world is an allegorical painting of Loyola. In the southwest a i s l e is an expressive fresco of the Kuttenbergers making money. The dress of the period is most accurately pourtrayed. Other frescoes discovered and preserved are of the F l a g e l l a t i o n, and the Crowning of Thorns, and Christ before Pilate.

Another interesting object in the church is a model of some miners in their long b l o u s e s, with peaked hood, kneeling with their lamps near a windlass. This commemorates the miraculous preservation of some miners who were buried in the mines, and lost; but they prayed to St. Barbara, and found a passage opened to them, that led them to an exit; and they issued from the earth near the church. We lingered in and about St. Barbara

PARADE COSTUME OF THE MINERS AT KUTTENBERG.

for a very long while, to return to it again after visiting some of the sites of scenes whereon had been enacted some of the most terrible episodes of the awful fratricidal struggle of the Hussite period. It was here that John Hus, in 1409, heard King Wenzel's judgment against him, and his prophetic warning that he did not incur the 'proof of Fire.' Hus, says Palacky, left Kuttenberg nearly hopeless, and fell into so terrible a sickness that men doubted for his life.

In 1419, the miners of Kuttenberg, then the second town in Bohemia, were the most terrible enemies of the Chalicers, as the more moderate of the two Hussite parties were called.   The name refers to their belief that the laity in the Communion should take both the bread and wine. Leave was given to kill Hussites without trial, and a reward offered of one schock of groschen (*i.e.* sixty shillings) for a lay heretic, and five schock for a Hussite priest ; and this had the effect of making the prisoners so numerous, that some were burnt, others beheaded, and others thrown down the pit shafts. Man hunts were organised, and within a short time 1600 were done to death.   So savage and relentless became the fiendish work, that the wretched Hussites were leashed together in gangs, driven to the pit's mouth, the first one or two driven over, and then all soon followed, dragged on by their falling brethren, hurtling against the pit shaft until their bruised corpses lay in a heap at the pit's bottom. One of the mines where such awful scenes of murder were enacted was that of St. Martin's ; and we made our way out of the town up the hill to this St. Martin's Schacht.   It lies just under the Kohlenberg, or Kank, or Gangberg, and we found the mine had lately been re-opened, and there was the windlass and the lantern, as in the model of five hundred years ago ; and far down in the dark depths we could hear the click, click of the

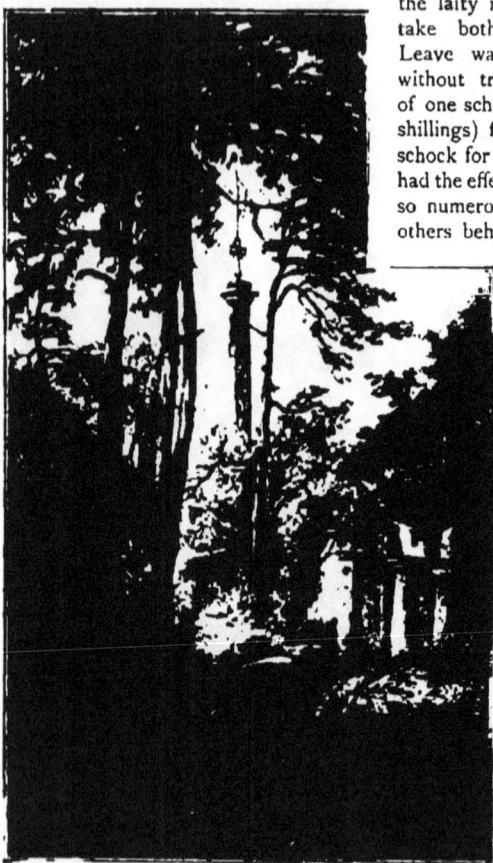

THE MONUMENT TO THE HUSSITES, KUTTENBERG.

miner's hammer. The mine is now some three hundred feet deep, and good ore of silver is got from it; but our thoughts were on the scenes of five centuries since, when history asserts that no less than 5496 human beings were hurled down this shaft. We went on up to the Kahlenberg, now called the Kankberg, amid old mine heaps and mine shafts to this historic hill. This hill has now been bought from Graf Chotek, and is a park for the Kuttenbergers; from it is a wide view; Prague lies far away north-west, Tabor south-west, and beneath is the village of Kank. The sound of the bells of Kuttenberg came out to us, and no more warlike sounds than the bark of a dog ascended to the hill, and that was mingled with the hum of insects and chirp of birds; butter-flies flew beneath the strong-scented pines, and all was peace on this hill where such horrible cruelties had been done in the name of holy Church five centuries since, when this hill was saturated with martyrs' blood. A monument is on the hill with an inscription to 'God's fighters, by God's help and hope from Him that we may conquer with Him.' This is in memory of all those who died for freedom's sake in 1419–21. All down the hill-side are the *klufts*, or shafts, where so many perished, and to the south-east is the village of Sedlec, where may be seen some terrible relics of Wycliffe days, for here on this pleasant hill all the terror is gone, and memory alone recalls its horrors. The church of Kank has many points of interest.

Sedlec, though now a very quiet place, is of greater antiquity than Kuttenberg, and can boast an appearance in history in 1142. Its great church is a very strange building, with a triple west door, having three baldachins over it, with three statues. It has four aisles, and these are carried round to the *ambulatoire* of the choir, producing a good effect. The pillars have a swelling in the centre, as some Eastern work, and the capitals are very quaint; in the choir they are floreated. A curious stair-way leads up to the gallery of the transept, from whence the work of the builder can well be examined. There is a curious Magdalene in the Lady chapel, a modern lady in black evening dress. This is the more noticeable, as in Bohemia the Roman Catholic churches are excessively plain, and have very few of the tinselled gewgaws and dressed dolls so common in the south of Europe. Rome appears to have been careful not to have too hastily altered the appearance of the churches of the followers of Hus. The confessional stalls are good carved and inlaid work, and the choir stalls freely carved with arabesques and cupids of the Renaissance period. This latter work was done in the adjoining Cistercian monastery, that is now one of the largest tobacco factories in Austria, employing some two thousand workers. So have the uses of the building changed.

From this curious and interesting building we walked on, under sweet-smelling trees, with chestnut and fruit-trees in full bloom, and with oxen lowing around us, to a flowering hop-garden. The warm sun shone in the foliage and on the flowers; all was full of warmth and life and beauty;

but on reaching the door of the chapel, which now stands in this hop-garden, a terrible sight meets the eye: down in the semi-dark chapel great trophies, and pillars, and pyramids of skulls and bones are dimly seen. Everything is made of human bones. Even the candelabra are of small bones. The coat-of-arms of the Rosen-bergs, with the rose, so suggestive of our Tudor rose, is of bones, an I.H.S. hung from the roof is worked in human bones. There is a scent of death in this half-underground, dimly-lit chapel, and a sense of horror creeps over one as we look around at these sad remnants of mortality piled on all sides. The Schwarzen-berg arms, with the historic Turk's head, is also worked out in bones. And great pyramids of skulls are piled up fifteen feet square at the base. A great candelabra of chains of bones and skulls hangs down from the centre of this build-ing, and on the altar are lines of skulls, all with gashes in them, where the murderous weapons have done their work.

INTERIOR OF SEDLEC CHAPEL.

It was with an intense relief we ascended again out into the soft warm air, so full of beauty and life, from this sombre charnel-house and proof of what the struggle for the world's freedom had cost Bohemia, and—awful reminder that the world has not yet learnt the Christ-like rule of love—there came marching past a regiment of soldiers with bugles playing.

Instinctively, after wandering over the scenes where such terrible deeds had been done, and after looking probably at the sad remains of some who had suffered through those deeds, the question flew to our lips, Were there still any followers of Hus and Wyclif in this neighbourhood? and our old friend Mathias Seffler, who was accompanying us, told us there were about two thousand Protestants in the villages around, Lutherans and Augsburgers.

There is much more to be seen in Kuttenberg, but we can only speak of one church that every Englishman should reverence; for beneath its roof the 'Great Forgotten Englishman,' Peter Payne, the link between Wyclif and Luther, presided over the last great assembly of Hussites in Bohemia. For two hundred years less one, Protestants worshipped in this church largely through the power and influence of our countryman Peter Payne; and it is strange to enter the church to-day and note the almost entire absence of the usual, to our eyes superstitious, decorations of a Roman Catholic church. All is most plain, but the building is a fine one and little altered since the 6th of July, 1444, when Payne spoke with such force amidst its pillars, that the Council was dissolved, lest his words should convince too many of his truth and faith.

A drive that repaid us amply in calm pleasure and historic knowledge, was one taken to seek for any remnants of that town of a year, Sion. All told us, even our editor friend, Gustav Touzil, that naught was left of its walls and defences, but with Mr. Mathias Seffler as guide we drove in the direction where history said the town had been built, and on a wooded hill-top, hid by undergrowth, we discovered the foundations of the walls and traces of the building. The vallum also around the hill town, where it was not too steep and precipitous for assault, was also still remaining.

Kuttenberg in old days was a favourite residence of emperors and kings. It was from here that the leader of the Taborites, Zizka, drove King Sigismund, and Kuttenberg was afterwards a favourite town of King George of Podiebrad. Its inhabitants of to-day reverence its past vigorous history, and their schools and institutions show an intellectual life that is yet full of vigour and provocative of much thought to a stranger. And if we have lingered longer over it than over some other towns of equal size, it is because within and around it centres so much of the stormiest periods of the history of their country, for which the Kuttenbergers have so strong a patriotic love.

From Kuttenberg a convenient railway runs viâ Kolin and Podiebrad to Prague. At Kolin the Elbe is crossed, and this busy commercial town can be visited in the steps of Carlyle, who came here to visit the battle-field where Frederick the Great was surprised by Marshal Daun; but although it goes back into the fifteenth century, Kolin has not the interest of so many other towns in Bohemia, and so we move onwards to Podiebrad, that lies in the middle of a great plain, all rich with fruit-trees that seem to stretch away in the far distant circle of blue mountains. Here at once is seen the great square castle with its tower rising above the plain, where was born the famous defender of the Hussites, George of Podiebrad. In 1352 this castle was in the possession of Bocek of Kunstat, whose son was a great friend and supporter of Hus. It was in 1420 King George was born here, and from here in 1448 that he started forth against Prague and overthrew the powerful Rosenbergs.

KANK CHURCH.

PRAGUE.

THE GRABEN, PRAGUE.

CHAPTER VI.

PRAGUE.

ALL life in Prague centres round the Carls Bridge, just as in Athens the traveller hastens on his arrival to climb the Acropolis, and returns again and again to look out from amidst its temples over modern Athens, so in Prague the Carls Bridge draws all visitors to its statued arches, there to look around at the city, with its towers, and pinnacles, and clustered buildings, stretching away on either side of the swift-rushing Moldau. But although the Carls Bridge cannot claim the antiquity of the Acropolis, yet it not only represents a great dead past, but it still is the centre of all the busy life in Prague of to-day.

The Moldau divides Prague, or Praha, as the Cechs call it, into two distinct portions, a division that in old days has ofttimes divided the town against itself, king or emperor holding the one part, and the people the other. As we emerge from the narrow streets of the old town that lie on the east side of the Moldau, and ascend the steep slope that leads up to the bridge, the grand, high-peaked roofed tower of the old gateway, with its coloured shields and statues, strikes most picturesquely ; and as we pass beneath its arch, with the busy crowd coming and going, the glimpse

beyond of the opposite part of the town, the Kleinseite (or Littleside) is
most impressive.

Across the bridge the long lines of statues stretch. Beyond is the
great western bridge tower, and above it, climbing in irregular beauty, the
towers, and green domes, and pinnacles of church and castle and cathedral.
The crowd seem hurrying and hastening as any modern crowd ; but as one
nears the two great central groups of the Crucifixion, it is strange to notice
that all passers-by, with but few exceptions, raise the hat and cross themselves ; and still stranger is it to notice that many at another point place

VIEW FROM CARLS BRIDGE, PRAGUE.

the hand hurriedly upon the parapet, and drawing it forward, then again
cross themselves. At this latter spot a brass cross with double arms,
worn smoothly by millions of fingers, is seen let into the parapet ; and this
adjoins the statue to the St. John of Nepomuc, whose statue now replaces
that of John Hus, and whose body, when thrown into the swift rushing
Moldau, according to the legend, lay beneath this arch in spite of current,
awaiting its withdrawal. Be this as it may, the peasantry now adore the
Holy Jan whom the Roman Catholic Church, in her crafty wisdom, has given
them to replace the Holy Jan Hus who for two hundred years was
revered and adored. In many places we shall see the statue of Hus

turned into the statue of Jan of Nepomuc, by adding the five-starred halo to the figure.

But round this statue on the Holy Jan's Day, May 16, surges a crowd of singing, praying pilgrims, that is full of rich colour and quaint costume. From all parts of the varied empire of Austria they come in all garbs ; a little chapel is erected around the statue, and mass is said on the bridge, the peasants singing and joining in the responses most melodiously, and with a strange, powerful pathos that moves even to tears. Then all the streets of Prague are filled with pilgrims, who camp on the church steps, and it is no difficult stretch of the imagination to feel that life has stepped backward into the Middle Ages.

Although this bridge has been the centre of life in Prague for nine hundred years (there was a wooden bridge here in the twelfth century, this present bridge, as its name shows, was built by Carl IV. in 1357), yet the earliest buildings in Prague are upon a height farther down the river at the Wyschehrad. Here commenced the history not only of Prague, but of Bohemia.

The earliest known inhabitants of Bohemia were the Bojen, a famous branch of the Keltic or Gallic race, so writes Palacky ; then came the Markomannen, and these conquering into Italy were driven back until, in the year 172, the Romans penetrated Bohemia, built fortresses, and manned them with warriors. At the Schlossberg, near Kamnitz, are some doubtful traces of Roman work. Crushed and defeated by the invading Huns, the Markomannen race gave place to the Slav-Cechs, who have ever since possessed the land ; but with a large admixture of Teutonic inhabitants that ever leads to much race hatred. Where the Slav-Cechs came from is a disputed point, and has never been settled ; but upon the Cech of to-day, with dark thin hair and with faces of an Eastern type, the East seems indelibly printed. The name Cech, Palacky ascribes to a Croatian warrior of that name, who, in the second half of the fifth century, swept over Bohemia and conquered the remaining Boii and Markomannen, after Attila's fierce onslaught ; and in 627 these Slavs elected Samo, who had freed them from surrounding tribes, as their king, and thus, with the Wyschehrad as his principal seat, he established the first Slav kingdom that history recognises. Legend ascribes the founding of Prague itself, or at least a castle on the Hradschin, to Libusa, the daughter of Krok, a successor of Samo, who fetched Premysl, the lord of Stodic, literally from the plough to be her consort. He was ploughing when Libusa's messengers arrived offering her hand, and the kingdom of Bohemia. Her commands to build a castle above where now stands the Carls Bridge spanning the Moldau, tradition assigns to the eighth century ; but actual history is silent upon Bohemia from the middle of the seventh century, until the crowning of Charlemagne in 800 ; and of his struggles with the Bohemians we have already spoken, and must leap back from these days of tradition and myth into the present, and look out from the walls of the Wyschehrad of to-day, and revel in the view that lies before us. The rock on which stood the first castle goes steep down into the Moldau, and beyond the river is the flat plain away to the Weissberg of Schmichov, and to the right beyond this rise up the towers of the Hradschin, the cathedral dominating the towers and pinnacles of castle, church, and bridge. In the Kaiserwiese, or Emperor's meadows below, ofttimes the enemy has encamped against the force assembled on this height, and ofttimes has this Wyschehrad been held by one party, whilst the Hradschin has been in the possession of a foe. People against emperor, Hussite against Papist.

In the Church of SS. Peter and Paul that stands on this height within the walls is an interesting picture of the Wyschehrad in earlier times, with its walls and houses and domes, nearly all of which are now swept away.

Not far from here is the Karlshof Church, not much visited, but of curious interest. It is an octagonal dome, the largest Gothic dome known, and of graceful proportions. The groins spring from the pillar capitals and long corbels to the roof, which is groined in geometrical pattern. An apse of early English type is run out

THE TEINKIRCHE, PRAGUE (OLD HUSSITE CHURCH).

at the east side. The church of which this is the remains was built by Carl IV. in 1350.

Beyond these objects of interest there is not much in this part of Prague to detain one, but a pleasant walk past the new Bohemian Museum, and through the gardens, and down the broad Wenzel Platz, brings us back into the old town. Along the Graben we pass, once, as the name denotes, the moat of the town, now a broad handsome street, until on the left hand rises up the rich and splendid gateway known as the Powder Tower, grand relic of Prague's mediæval days, built in the year 1475, in the style with the high-pitched roof so peculiar to Prague, and well restored in the last decade.

Passing beneath this tower we are in the narrow tortuous streets of the old town, and the Zeltner Gasse leads us quickly into the Ring, the great Ring, into which have poured turbulent mobs and excited religionists, hot with passion against trick of Sigmund the word-breaker, or ruse of Pope, to again take from them the Chalice, the cup of the Sacrament.

Much of mediæval appearance is still preserved to this Ring, in spite of siege and storm and fire; and the old verses written against Prince Korybut best bring up the type of scenes witnessed in this open space in Hussite days. Then, as now, the towers of the Tein Church rose up on one side of the square, and the towers of the Rathhaus stood at the opposite corner; and as we look round on the old houses and towers, the bells of the Tein Church ring out, and the words of the old song strike forcibly with their rhythm :

> 'They bid ring the bells from the towers on high,
> And the folk all flocked to the Tein hard by;
> Not long did the priests in the church there stay,
> But streamed to the Ring in the light of day.
> And they cried aloud with fearful cries:
> "Beloved, we're threatened ! To arms ! Arise !"
> And the streaming folk then quickly knew,
> With treacherous letters they had to do.'

Often had the folk flocked to the Tein Church in crowds, during the agitated times when Wyclif's teaching was penetrating into the heart of Bohemia, and for more than two hundred years this church was the chief church of those who persisted in their right to take the sacrament of bread and wine. The west front of the church is half hid by the old Tein School, and above this is a niche where now stands a statue of the Virgin Mary. Formerly there stood there a gigantic gilt chalice, and beneath it the statue of George of Podiebrad. The interior is of rather poor architecture, but redolent of the stormy past; and to watch the mass being celebrated here, is to sit in the presence of the spirits of a fiery, agitated age. The great Hussite preacher, Archbishop Rockycana, continuously preached here, and his pulpit, though restored, still stands in the church.

On the opposite side of the picturesque square rises the tower of the old Town Hall and Council Chamber, and on its walls the immense old clock that was originally placed there in 1490. It proves that our telegraph clock of one to twenty-four hours is by no means a new idea; for this clock strikes the hours as we now have them, in the old Bohemian fashion of one to twenty-four. The clock, with its moving figures and pictures, is curious in other ways, and if the tourist is standing before it on a great *fête* day, when the square is filled with pilgrims in strange and varied costumes, he can well carry himself back in thought to the day four hundred years ago, when this clock began to tick forth the seconds.

On such a day, here may be seen mingling amidst a modern crowd, pedlars with their long coats, and dark hair flowing over their shoulders ; g r o u p s of women in brilliant-coloured head - dresses, sitting on the s t e p s ; knots of men from Moravia in short white jackets, with red collars and red great bobs to the lappels, and high jack-boots ; others with orna- mented vests, and embroidered breeches, and full white shirt sleeves, the white shirt coming out full below the vest, and beneath which is a broad band of some bright colour. Pilsen women are there, perchance, in blue bodices with mauve- coloured dress, black head- dress with red bands, bright blue stockings, and top-boots ; or some from Taus in rich b l a c k velvet jackets, with slashed sleeves, and a mass of distended red petticoats, quilted somewhat like the Greeks' fus- tenella. Other men have long white coats and blue trousers ; the older men with their long white hair falling over their shoulders, proving them verit- able pilgrims and wayfarers in this varied world. One tall handsome fellow we saw stand-

THE TOWN HALL ON THE RINGPLATZ, PRAGUE.

ing amidst a group below this old clock-tower, wore high jack-boots with tight close-fitting breeches, a slight vest, open in front and embroidered down the back with purple flowers ; the lappels of this were thrown open, showing the white shirt, the full sleeves of which were snowy white ; around his waist he wore a wide band with a brilliant-coloured cloth thrust into it, and on his

Group of peasants at Prague on St. John's Day.

[From a drawing by Walter Crane.

G

head a tight-fitting astrachan cap, from which uprose a long straight white feather. Near this young wrestler—for his tall feather proved his prowess in the wrestling ring, and it was seen above the crowd whenever he moved—was a young girl, straight as an arrow, with a many-coloured head-dress wound gracefully round her bright fair hair, that descended in long plaits ending in bunches of particoloured ribbons to her ankles, that were encased in high boots ; her dress was of purple, but half hid by an apron of red and yellow, with white bands and pink edges, with white lace around it. Below the dress, which reached to the knees, appeared her red and white ringed stockings ; and as she bore herself upright and gracefully, we linked her with him of the tall feather, for no romance writer had ever more picturesque figures for a mediæval romance. All these people, and many another picturesque group, were seen in and around this Ring-platz in May, 1890, on St. John's Day, that is on May 16, and their dress refutes the statement that picturesque and representative costume is not now to be met with in Europe.

Many of the rooms in the Council House are quaint, especially the old Council Chamber, and the antiquary and historian will be tempted to while away much time within its walls ; or, if he is favoured with a sight of them, over its rich archives. But we must leave the Ring-platz, and passing through the Nicholas-platz, giving a peep into the new Russian church that stands here, pass on, as many an excited crowd has done in days gone by, through the narrow streets, over the Carls Bridge into the Kleinseite, where is clustered a group of famous buildings. At the summit of them is the Cathedral, high up on the Hradschin, which is really the Acropolis of Prague ; though for reminiscence, and from a historical point of view, we have likened the Carls Bridge to it.

It was in the Court of the Archbishop Zbynek's palace in this Kleinseite that a historical scene took place. The Pope's bull against the heresies of Wyclif had been read in Prague. Seventeen of his books were condemned ; the archbishop threatened with the Church's curse all those who retained them. Hus took his Wyclif's works to the archbishop, with the request he should read them, and point out the errors in them ; but Zbynek was too wary to accept the challenge. Two hundred of the books were collected ; but at the instigation of the University the precious volumes were for a short time saved by King Wenzel, suggesting the burning should be put off until the Markgrave Jost came to Prague. Now Hus had given a copy of the *Trialogus*, which he had translated, to this Markgrave, and he was known as a lover of books. So Zbynek made haste to act, in spite of protestations from the University, and a special request from Hus and seven other members of the University, that a new appeal should be sent to the new Pope, Johann XXIII. He called together the prelates and clergy of Prague in his courtyard, surrounded them with a strong guard, piled up the books of Wyclif in their midst, and whilst *Te Deum laudamus*

was being chanted, set fire to them.   All the bells of Prague clanged with
a knell, to tell the people of the event, a knell that foretold the death of
Papal power in Bohemia for two centuries, a knell that gave fiery life to
the words of the burnt volumes.   This is one of the many famous scenes
which have occurred on this imperial part of old Prague.

The Cathedral, that crowns all the buildings on this height, can be
gained by passing through the Burg or Castle, a great range of buildings
with many courts and halls, and pictures and relics of past history.   From
the windows of the Maria Theresen Stift is a most excellent view of
Prague, its domes and towers, the winding Moldau with its bridges and
islands, and just beneath is the old palace of Wallenstein, with its dormer
windows.

The oldest church in Prague lies between the Burg and the Cathedral;
it is dedicated to St. George, and was built in 916, its round pillars have
great square capitals, and the 'dog's tooth' ornament is noticeable on some
of the arches.   The crypt is of good Romanesque work, but has been
painted white.   From this ancient church the Cathedral, that has suffered so
much from fire, can be visited, and although so much has been destroyed,
yet much remains that awakens keen interest.   The foundation stone of this
building was laid in 1344, but it has not yet been finished.   It is after the
style of Cologne, and the choir is a rich example of late Gothic work.   At
the back of the high altar is a curious wood carving that gives a good idea
of Prague as it was nearly three hundred years ago.   Stags are feeding
beneath the towers of the Hradschin, the Cathedral apse is as it now is,
and below is pictured the river with rafts upon it, and the dam across with
the break in the centre for the rafts to pass, as now; the Carls Bridge
stretches across it, but without the groups of figures that now so add to its
picturesqueness.   This carving represents the flight of King Frederick from
Prague in 1620.

There are nine chapels, that of St. John of Nepomuc contains his silver
shrine with a relief, showing the saint being thrown over the bridge into the
river; the shrine is said to contain a ton and a half of silver.   But the most
interesting chapel is that of St. Wenzel.   Like some other chapels we shall
see in Bohemia, the walls are lined with cut Bohemian precious stones, the
spaces between being of gold.   Above these frescoes of scenes of the life of the
saint are painted.   On the door of the chapel is the great Sanctuary knocker
with the Lion's head, to which St. Wenzel clung when murdered by his brother;
it was brought here from Old Bunzlaw, where the deed was done.

But we must quit the Cathedral, and cross again to the Burg to visit
the Wratislaw Hall and its adjoining chambers.   In this hall formerly the
newly crowned kings of Bohemia received homage, a ceremony the Cechs
are struggling to have re-established; and here the coronation feasts were held,
and on other occasions tournaments, though the hall seems small for that

purpose. The pillars are worth noticing, the mouldings are intertwined and twisted up to pointed ovals, working to central bosses; and in the Landtagssaal adjoining, the old ceiling is of curious design.

In a lesser room above this occurred the memorable deed that brought about the Thirty Years' War. From the east window of this room in the year 1618, the two royal councillors and their secretaries were thrown in hot passion down into the garden some fifty feet below, escaping death, it is said, by falling on a dung heap. From this window is a most lovely view of Prague far below, and as one looks down into the little garden, and sees the two monuments erected to commemorate the fact that the councillors were not killed, one marvels at the fact.

This mode of wreaking their passion on obstinate councillors was historic in Prague; for just 200 years before, in 1419, a crowd of enraged Hussites had stormed the Rathhaus of the Neustadt, and thrown seven of King Wenzel's new anti-Hussite councillors from the windows. This occurred at almost the other end of Prague, on the opposite side of the Moldau towards the Wyschehrad, on the great open space of the Carls-platz where stood the Rathhaus of the Neustadt or Newtown.

Below us, not far from the Kleinseite Ring, another picturesque open space, clustered round with fine buildings, is the old palace of the Wallensteins. This palace was built for the famous duke by an Italian architect, and is a fine example of domestic architecture. The great hall that runs the whole length of the palace is decorated with frescoes upon the ceiling representing the triumph of Wallenstein. Wallenstein's astrological chamber recalls Schiller's scenes in which Ceni the astrologer takes part. From this palace, up through the Thun Street, and on up past the Schwarzenberg Palace (the great descendants of the Rosenbergs, whose castles and palaces we shall visit in South Bohemia), we can pleasantly reach the Strahof Monastery, which well repays a visit. The church of the monastery is highly ornamented and painted, and rather striking in effect, reminding one somewhat of the Annunziata at Genoa. The tomb of Pappenheim, the great general of the Thirty Years' War, is here, and in the abbey itself are preserved rich collections of books, and missals, and manuscripts, and some good pictures, as well as, to the student of Bohemian history, important and large collections of the arms of most of the Bohemian families. From the great terrace of the abbey is a lovely view of the Hradschin, the cupola and tower of the Cathedral on the left, and beneath the massive square Burg, and below this runs the wide river with its green heights and islands intersecting the stream; and on either side of it, the town, with spires and pinnacles and towers, all of varied shapes, and the one dome of St. Nicholas; whilst just beneath us, as we stand in this quiet terrace, are orchards in full bloom, the fresh green trees sloping up the hillside to the little tower spires amidst the bright green leaves of the wooded hill opposite, from whence come the full rich song of blackbirds, and the softened chant of children singing in a school hard by.

After such a restful moment we leave the monastery and walk on round the fortress, and watch the soldiers at work and at drill, round to the Belvedere, a spot well deserving its name. The building is an old pleasure palace of Ferdinand I., a square building with a rich inflated copper roof, that gives the verdigris green that is so effective amidst other architectures. It is a fine example of Italian Renaissance, with columns running round it, and connected with these is a balcony, from which perhaps a finer view of the Hradschin is had than that looked upon from Strahof. At least it is different, and the round towers and crenulated walls, the Dom spires and pinnacles, and the two spires of St. George, form an extremely pretty view, and the great fosseway beneath is bright with trees, that are full of singing birds; and from here the view is extended to up the river, where are white cliffs and green islands. Within the buildings are fourteen large frescoes of the important events in Bohemian history, from 871 to 1790, and facing it is the pleasant Volksgarten, where good music can be enjoyed.

STATUE OF CHARLES IV., PRAGUE.

Ere quitting this side of Prague, the old Benedictine abbey in Brevnov, about half an hour's walk from the Hradschin, should be visited for its historic interest and pleasant situation, founded in 993. It was rebuilt in the seventeenth century; the church near it was built in 1706, to commemorate the terrible crushing of Protestantism at the Battle of the White Mountain.

So long we have wandered amidst the buildings and gardens on this western portion of Prague, of the Kleinseite and Hradschin; but we must descend from its heights, leaving yet many a church and cloister, garden, museum, and palace unvisited, and by a pleasant road down amid the old fortification descend to the small chain bridge, and cross over to the handsome building of the Rudolfinum that lies in a fine open space well laid out with trees and flowers. This very new-looking part of Prague is close to the very oldest part of the city, at least in appearance, for just beyond the open space narrow streets lead into the Josephstadt, the Ghetto of Prague.

The Rudolfinum is a remarkably handsome building of classic architecture, and housed within its walls are some fine examples of modern sculpture by native sculptors, a large collection of pictures, including examples by the well-known Bohemian artist Gabriel Max, whose cottage we saw at Hammer. It also devotes space to a library, and to a music *Conservatoire*, which has a fine concert hall. The energy of modern life in Bohemia is well epitomised here, where music, painting, sculpture, and industry find a common home.

From this bright building and free open space, a short dive down Josephstown Street, and, by another of the sudden changes we are in the narrow, high-housed, dirty, sordid streets of an old Jewish town. All the names are Cohens, and Levis, and Samuels, and the old men pass by in long coats and with long curled grey hair; and as we enter the narrow street of the Rabbis, the curious affection of the Jew for old clothes and boots and shoes is marked by the shops; but a short way down this street and we see the old Jewish Council House, with a clock with a Hebrew and a Christian dial plate, then up a narrow street on the left, and we enter one of the strangest spots in Europe.

Out of the dirt and filth of the narrow streets into this may-tree shaded, silent burial-place, where stone touches stone, and where the buried dead laid, are as is the Jewish custom, one above the other, in new layers of earth, without moving or disturbing where the past dead are buried; here they lie in their silent resting-place far above the level upon which their synagogue was built.

Many of these old crowding, clustering stones have the signs of the tribes upon them. The hands of Aaron, the cup of Levi, the stag, the fish, the double triangle, David's sign. Many of the stones are inscribed in

Hebrew, and the Jews' tradition says this synagogue and burial-place was founded by a company that fled from the destruction of Jerusalem by Titus. The oldest date on the stone is 606, so we were told, and we let the statement stand. The quiet of the spot under the fresh scented trees, is a strange contrast to the narrow, vilely odorous streets near it; its size has been exaggerated by some writers, its area embraces a hectare and a quarter, that is about three acres.

The old synagogue near it was rebuilt in about 1142, when the earlier synagogue was burnt down; now it is a strange little spot supported by two pillars octagonal in shape. It is divided into two aisles or rather naves, around it are little windows, through which the women can see the service; they cannot hear or join in the prayers, and, we are told, as the service was conducted in Hebrew—the old tongue—there was no necessity for their hearing, each could pray for themselves.

Not far from this old synagogue is the so-called new one, now used—and a service in it is a strange sight. The men stand in high hats with the talitha or prayer scarf round their shoulders; some with gold and black ornamentations; the fast reading of the Books of Moses, the quick response, and the calling out of the objects of charity, to which the surrounding men bid the amount they will give, so curiously suggestive of an auction, is one of those strange sights that live in the memory. They have no objection to visitors even moving round the synagogue during service; in fact, motioned us to pass around on one occasion, but hats must be kept on. A little walk in and out the alleys around these old buildings shows the life of the poor Jew of Prague; now and then the bright pretty face of a young Jewish girl is seen, but vice and crime with its sordid accompaniment of dirt and filth, and money clutching in petty ways, predominate in Josephstown; and one is glad to pass up the Geist Gasse into the old Ring, and breathe again a wider, fresher air.

And after some hours spent in the Ghetto, a stroll is agreeable down to the river past the Carls and Franzens bridges, and across to the Sophien island, where on summer afternoons and evenings most excellent bands play good music. Here on a soft evening the Praguers come to sup and listen to the music, or to enjoy a dance. Bright waltzes, or crashing marches, or classic and modern *morceaux*, lend vivacity and beauty to a gay scene, and in similar gardens and halls in other parts of the town are found places of entertainment for all grades of the populace. The Bohemian is a passionate musician, and the poor factory worker, after his eleven or twelve hours' work, may be seen enjoying a penny glass of the common light beer, and swaying his head to some exciting harmonies by Dvorak, their famous countryman.

The Cech's love of their country and of its history is exemplified also in their magnificent and spacious museums, especially the great new

Bohemian Museum that is close to the Stadt Park, not far from the railway station. To just hint at the interesting objects preserved in the Prague museums, we may mention examples of the precious stones yielded by the mountains : black amber, pure gold, diamonds, opals, chalcedony from the Iser, and large garnets ; Missals, and early printed books, and curious historical paintings, such as one of Prague in 1606 and 1685, before and after the Thirty Years' War. In the first the Wysehrad is destroyed, in the second rebuilt. Prague Bibles of 1480, and one in Cech of 1500 ; the Psalter of the Utraquist, with the burning of Hus illuminated ; the Psalter of the Hussites of Tabor ; the War Song of the Hussites, beginning, 'Ye who are God's warriors,' and documents in Hus' hand-writing, a fine clear decided hand ; horn goblets and cups of tenth and eleventh centuries, as well as interesting prehistoric collections.

If the national museums are full of rich historic objects, there is a lesser museum that is most remarkable, as the outcome of the patriotic love of one man, who from small beginnings has at length built a really fine museum, and filled it with most interesting objects illustrative of Bohemian life. This man, Mr. Vojta Naperstek, by incessant work has amassed a curious collection ; and the rich costumes of the Bohemian peasantry especially can be studied here. Connected with this museum is an English and American reading-room, and not far from it stands the house wherein John Hus lived whilst preaching in Prague before Queen Sophie, and con-gregations intent upon hearing his new expositions of Scripture and of the teaching of the English master, Wyclif.

From this point the Palacky Bridge can easily be reached, that has been named after the indefatigable historian, who worked from March 1831 until 1866, to build up his monumental history of Bohemia. And in his ten volumes, or as he divides them, five volumes of one, two, or three parts each, he has written a work that is one of the greatest historical studies of our century, so minutely has he examined and verified original documents, and woven them into a picturesque whole, rich in exciting details, and diffuse upon important epochs.

Modern life in Prague is full of activity. If the traveller can penetrate into the factories, he will find the artisan abreast of the highest technical knowledge of the day, the streets are full of movement, and in the gardens and places of resort is much vivacious life ; but the passion for dancing here, as in other large towns, leads to much that is sad. In one busy centre we were told that this led also to much consumption, owing to the dancers coming out heated into the cold frosty air ; but the vice of drunkenness is very rarely in evidence. The amusements of the people are generally rational and intellectual, neither besotted or inane ; and the tourist who has learnt to know Prague and its people will stand once more on the Carls Bridge, and will look round on all her towers and monuments, and he will feel somewhat of the passionate love with which her people reverence her past.

And thinking of the tempestuous past of storm and siege, persecution, and pest, and fire, that this old bridge has weathered, he will grasp somewhat the excitement and horror of the Praguers, when, in September, 1891, the floods bore down upon it with battering-rams of masses of timber, even as they had done for five centuries past, but this time with

RUINS OF PRAGUE BRIDGE DURING THE FLOOD IN 1891.

fatal effect, for great breaches were made in the solid masonry, and half the old bridge was swept away ; but, strange to say, St. John of Nepomuc was left uninjured, and belief in his power has thus been strengthened in the minds of the peasantry.

And here on the old bridge, now again restored, we take our last look at Prague, at her unique towers and clustering pinnacles, of bridge, and Burg, Cathedral, and Tein Church, a scene unsurpassed for interest and beauty in any city in Europe.

CARLSTEIN.

PILSEN.

CHAPTER VII.

CARLSTEIN AND PILSEN.

THE imperial castle of Carlstein plays so important a part in the history of Bohemia, and its story is so dwelt upon by Palacky, that we were anxious to stand within its walls, and it is well we did so on April 30, 1889. On leaving Carlstein station, a little inn on the right, with a pleasant terrace, gives a first peep of this stronghold, hidden in the recesses of surrounding hills, that rise to the heights of from a thousand to fifteen hundred feet. It is a strange disorganised mass of assembled buildings, irregular and bizarre, but yet massive, strength-suggesting, and standing up boldly on its rocky cone, defiant and very picturesque. From this view the little church of the village seems to form part of the great masses of masonry on the hill above, its red-domed tower adding to the picturesqueness of the red, grey, and yellow walls of the castle.

The isolated rock cone on which all this mass of masonry stands is wholly surrounded and even topped by other hills, but at a safe distance in the days of slings, or even arquebuses, the heavy stone shot would fall short or spent against the massive walls.

When we had been received by the castellan, and had climbed up the steep roadway within the first and second gate to the interior of the building, we found it in a state of semi-ruin and preparation for restoration ; but we were glad to look upon many parts of it yet untouched by the restorer's hands. We first entered the Knights' Chapel of St. Nicholas, a very tiny little church, and then passed up to the Emperor Carl IV.'s rooms. The audience room has some good panelling and a good ceiling, and some of the old weapons were retained here ; and from a balcony the occupants of these rooms could look out far down to the village of Budnan below. In the sleeping-room of Carl one window with a round head suggests the date of the building, and a secret stair leads from here to the great rooms where the guests were housed. Below these rooms were the three State prisons, and above them the dean's, or, as our guide told us, the archbishop's dwelling-rooms. The doors to the vaults have the peculiar shoulder-heads, with squared arch above, so often seen in these castles. A bridge leads across from the emperor's dwelling to the collegiate or Maria Chapel, and here some interesting frescoes are left of Carl and Blanche de Valois, and of Carl giving his son Wenzel a ring ; these, though painted in the fourteenth century, are in good preservation, and a cross of precious stones is also well preserved.

In passing from here by a narrow passage the diminutive, minute St. Catherine's Chapel is reached. This tiny church, really in the castle wall, has been a rude gem of rich decorations ; formerly 1049 precious stones lined its walls, encircled by gold ; seventy-two of these are left, one a great chalcedony. The little roof is groined from bosses ; the altar at the end and two chairs, one for the emperor to rest upon and the other for prayer, was its only furniture. Here he spent days in absolute solitude, prayer, and meditation. A hole in the wall admitted his slight food and important State documents. The door is of good iron work, painted ; the eagle and Bohemian lion alternating in diamonds, with the border between, formed of roses and crosses. Over the door is a good fresco of Carl and his wife Anna, each with crosses, and in an attitude of reaching forth their hands to each other, a rich cross being between them. Carl is represented with an old, worn face, dark full beard, and long flowing hair ; and there is still preserved here an expressive marble statue of the Virgin and Child, of Carl's time. The little window is of old glass, with burnt-in colour. A rude Crucifixion represents Christ on the cross being pierced, whilst a mediæval burgher-like soldier is on the right hand, and Mary, sorrowing and fainting, is being led away by St. John on the left ; and the Jews around are mocking Christ. Probably this is the tiniest chapel known, and certainly it must have been one of the richest in decoration.

From this chapel in the wall we went on to the Marie Chapel, all arcaded with frescoes, and from thence into the great five-storied square

ST. CATHERINE'S CHAPEL, CARLSTEIN.

tower that dominates all the buildings. Here, in what was pointed out to us as the Schwerere Gefangniss, we were told human bones had been lately found in the corner. In the lower storey was formerly a judgment chamber, and the stairway that leads to the upper rooms is most richly and interestingly illuminated with frescoes illustrating the life of St. Wenzel, and his grandmother Ludmilla. These frescoes, by Nicholas of Weimar, we saw amidst the dust of preparation for the general restoration of the castle, but untouched, and they deserve pages to their description ; and the castle is worthy a whole volume, but we can only hint at the type of scenes depicted. There is a good scene of a vineyard with wine-press, and mill, and men, and near this is the Baptism of Ludmilla. The saint is standing naked in a font, whilst a priest pours water over her from a great pitcher. She was baptised in 871, and was murdered later on by her daughter-in-law, who then incited her son, the heathen Boleslau, to murder his Christian brother Wenzel, which he did in the church at Old Bunzlau in 936. An excellent fresco of the murder is on this stairway, and we were tempted to halt here too long, but at length we passed on through various halls, astonished, in spite of the disorder that reigned amid the restoration preparations, and dust and dirt of neglect, at the rich work and former glories of this strange castle.

At length we came to three barred and bolted iron doors. What new surprise awaited us here pricked our imagination, as we waited for their opening. Through them we passed and stood in the Chapel of the Cross. A wonderful room or church, at first sight square, but as we passed in, we saw that a thin transept gave it the form of the cross ; but it was unlike any chapel our eyes had ever seen. The nave, or entrance, was spanned by a roof that sprang to a central boss, and its vault was coloured blue as the heavens, and flecked with stars of glass of burnt-in gold. In the little choir the dome was also flecked with stars, and with sun and moon ; and all the walls were inlaid with precious stones of irregular form, encircled by stamped gold, upon which were pressed varied designs. Formerly, over two thousand amethysts, jaspers, agates, and other precious stones adorned these walls, and above them are one hundred and twenty-six pictures of saints by Theodore of Prague, painted in the fourteenth century. The windows were of precious stones, some are still intact of topaz and amethyst, and the light through these is very soft and beautiful, the lead in which they are inclosed being pressed with gold.

The altar screen is of worked iron, and in it were hung precious stones ; one only hangs still in its place, to hint at the beauty of this screen in the past centuries. Over the altar is another rich, iron-decorated screen, and behind this were kept the crown jewels and Bohemia's treasure, hence the iron doors, and bolts, and nineteen locks ; and hence the position of this still maiden castle.

The whole chapel is most singularly fascinating, and we were thankful to thus stand in it before a finger of the restorer had tested if the gold, or the stars, or the precious stones were yet firmly in, enduring the ages. At one end of the chapel was placed a glass case of statuettes and ornamentations, that had been collected about the building. We had a look at these ere being ushered out through the iron doors, and carefully locked and bolted out of this sanctuary, our minds still filled with its strange, Eastern-like splendour; but not for long, for we were led up to the top of the tower, and our eyes were filled with the lovely view around.

Here we could see how well Carl had chosen the position of this castle, that was to contain all that Bohemia held most precious. On this entirely isolated cone, surrounded on all sides by uprising hills, as the central cone of a great volcanic crater, all preparations for attack could be seen and thwarted. As we looked around after standing in this chapel, where, five hundred years before, Carl had prayed and fasted, on all hands were soft wooded hills and rich vales. From this uppermost part of the castle we descended to the well-tower; a peasant woman came to draw water as we stood there, and whilst she was at the well we were shown some of the enormous stone balls, twelve to eighteen inches in diameter, which had been hurled at the castle in the Hussite siege; and as we passed up through the great gateways of the castle we were shown the old doors all pricked and scored with arrow-heads.

These actual marks and relics of the bygone age brought vividly back to us the scene of 1422, when the three hills around were full of the Prague army and their Polish allies, intent on capturing this castle and its treasure from Sigmund the Word-breaker.

The besiegers had cannon and powder, but if they put much powder in, the cannon burst, and if they put little in, the shot fell short; so the engines that did most damage were the old ballisters and catapults, those powerful slings that threw the heavy stone shot we saw laying about by the well.

The old well-tower was a special mark for the stone balls; for the well destroyed, a water famine would force the four hundred defenders to yield, and besides, it lay at the foot of the castle, and the stone balls fell heavily on it. So hot became the fire that the besieged slung up one of their powerful prisoners over it with a wisp in his hand, such as was used to drive away flies, to flick off the balls; this in derision at the little mischief done by these balls, and also with the hope that the Prague men would cease to shoot at their own friend. But so much the more did the shot hail around this unfortunate prisoner, until in mercy the castle men took him down, aye, and untouched, although he had hung there throughout the day. A glimpse this into these fighting days, that the arrow marks and broken battlements and bespotted windows helped us to realise.

It was nearly dark when we reached the village from whence we intended to take the night train to Pilsen ; but ere the train came we saw a sight that will long live in our memories.   On a distant hillside we suddenly saw a fire blaze out, and then another ; we pointed them out to a well-dressed villager, thinking some farm was on fire.   'Ah,' he exclaimed, ' *Die Hexen wird gebrant !* '   ' The witches are being burnt !' and soon on all the dark hills fires were lit up ; we saw comet-like flames dart through the air, and we heard cries, and shouts, and shrieks on the near hills ; and above us on the castle height burst out flames ; jovial peasants were driving the witches from their own village ; for, said our friend, ' if they don't make more noise the witches from the other villages will come here.'   The comet flames were besoms dipped in pitch, lit, and hurled blazing through the air.   Then

dawned the thought on us it was Wal-purgiss night, and ' this the way to outwit witches.'   The morning would dawn on May-day, and to-night the Judas coal must be buried, or the witches would do harm to the seed, unless this consecrated coal be hid in the earth ; the cross must be painted on the cattle stalls, or the cows would die or give blood for milk ; all brooms and rakes must be carefully looked after, lest the witches ride forth on them ; and the fires must flame forth, and incessant noise be kept up, or the driven witches would find a fateful home in some lazy village, doomed for one year to mishap and misfortune.   The obedience to this

WITCHES' FIRES.

superstition was being carried out on all the hills around us ; in some places we heard effigies of the witches were burnt, but we did not see them this time ; half in earnest, half in boisterous fun, is the custom kept up from heathen days ; but when we stood at the quiet little station it seemed incongruous to await a steam engine to take us away from Carlstein, where we had been living lost in the past.

But the train came at length, and with the witches' fires still burning around us we stood looking out on the dark hills ; and at midnight entered Pilsen.   The vigorous strains of a good band playing a march from *Carmen* awoke us on May-morning at six o'clock, and mingled with it was a succession of wave-sounds, as of the sea rising and falling ; and when we sallied out we found this came from the great market-place, that was crowded with people in strange costume of every shade of colour.   Above the gabled houses of the great open square rose the thin spire of the high-roofed church, and spread all over the square were booths, and sheds and waggons, with the patient oxen in them, and piles of vegetables, and cheeses, and dresses, and boots and shoes, and every commodity to satisfy the wants of man inwardly and outwardly.   Here were the market women in every conceivable colour, deep red predominating.   One old dame stood

PILSEN PEASANTS.

at a corner in low shoes, deep red stockings and red apron, and red head-dress, but with a black dress and with her basket *hutte* on her back piled up with vegetables, she made a charming study.   As in a kaleidoscope, the colours moved and shifted, and weaved themselves into strange com-binations.   Around a pile of eggs, and butter, and fowls, were grouped women in mauve, red, light pink, blue, chocolate, dark brown, olive. yellow, a black-grey alternating on one dress with yellow and red, very light blue,

THE MARKET-PLACE, PILSEN.

pink, purple, and primrose yellow. In another part of the square were piles of cakes of all colours like the dresses, and oranges and lemons, lettuce, and carrots, and flowers; beyond this were stalls hung with the brilliant coloured dresses, and near it stood a woman whose dress we give as an example of the rest. Her head was enveloped in light grey, she wore a black jacket, and a dress of reddish and grey stripes, with a double blue border; and behind a sash of deep red, yellow, and blue; and her feet were encased in very white stockings and low shoes. Another near her wore a primrose-yellow head-dress, a full white chemisette above bare arms, a bright pink apron, and grey dress, with deep red stockings. The strangest dress was distended masses of red petticoats, that as the women moved or stooped showed fold on fold, as the Greek *fustenella*, of this brilliant red; moving about amidst these masses of varying shifting colour, we felt a supreme pity for those who say costume has died out in Europe. We took notes of half-a-dozen other combinations of costume, but have no room for more. From these imagine the crowd filling this market-square.

Passing amidst these parti-coloured peasants, we entered the great church in the centre of the Platz, and found it to be of good Decorated architecture, with the peculiarity that the groining of the roof sprang clear from the pillars without the usual break of capitals. There was the usual absence of gewgaws and trinkets, but some good altar pictures. The church was built in 1292.

Pilsen is associated with the mighty Duke of Friedland, Wallenstein, and the dark complot that led to his murder at Eger. In the high square house or palace, with its little domed turret and Decorated front, may be seen the room where Piccolomini and Isolani, and the other generals, signed the conspiracy against Wallenstein.

Most of the museums in even the smallest towns of Bohemia are of interest. The town clerks, or the curators, take an intelligent and learned interest in the history and capabilities of their country, and arrange and classify their collections with care. Here, in Pilsen, were some objects of great historic value: the bull of excommunication of George of Podiebad, the gold seal of Sigismund of 1434, and of John of Luxemburg of 1320. Examples of the earliest printing in Bohemia, in 1467, said our guide; but as it is stated that the first Bohemian printing-press was set up in Pilsen in 1468, and the *History of Troy* was the first work printed, we wanted confirmation of the 1467 date, but were unable to satisfy ourselves, although we were again assured that date was correct. There is also preserved in this museum a little collection of weapons of past days. The flails and morning stars, and some Hussite balls, and some Hussite money with Hus's image, and a collection of stone, bronze, and iron articles, that were found all together in the same grave: a puzzle for archæologists. Some interesting fibulæ with the sun and swan upon them, and to come down to a much later date, some uniforms that were worn when Vienna was captured by the Turks, only two centuries since, are here preserved.

It is noteworthy how the Pilseners have preserved a record of their history in the names of their streets. There is Premysl Street and Hus Street, Podiebrad and Rosenberg, and to come to Bohemia's modern literature, Havilicek Street; and to commemorate their famous indefatigable

PILSEN COSTUMES.

historian, Palacky Place and Street; and it was whilst strolling amid these streets, calling up memories of Bohemia's stormy history, that we were halted by noting preparations for a funeral. All grades in Bohemia make much of the burying of their dead, and be it in city or on the forest-clad mountain-side, a funeral is an impressive and ofttimes touching scene; or even an elaborate pageantry. Here, before a suburban house, waited a great silver car, with torches burning around it. Grey horses were harnessed

WOMEN OF PILSEN.

to it, decked in blue trappings; and before this was another car of silver, hid with great wreaths of beautiful flowers, and with palms and streaming broad ribbons : the coffin was white, with a silver cover, and wreathed with palms. The priest, dressed in black velvet, bore a lighted candle in his hand, and was followed by two acolytes. Behind the hearse came the mourners : a group of officers, one of the general staff, with green plumes, and a company of soldiers; and four young girls, walking erect, but showing how great was the effort that bore them so erect. A mother, in deep black, leant on a stalwart son ; and as the brilliant and sombre procession moved away from the dead man's home, the military band burst forth with a crash, that faded away into a soft, piteous tearful wail, that in its tenderness forced tears from many an eye. Behind the chief mourners fell in a great mass of town-folk, rich and poor; the near friends in black, the poor in their bright head-dresses ; and out trailed the procession through the town, and on its outskirts halted on a little bridge over a river, where stood a cross and figure of the Virgin with the dead Christ. Here, with the hearse and coffin before the cross, the priest read forth some prayers, and the scene upon this high little narrow bridge, with the river with its bordering willows beneath, and behind, the town, from whence came out the sound of the tolling bells, from the uplifting towers to this varied group of mourners before the old cross, was most impressive and touching. The prayers ended, the sad wail of music rose most softly, and then, as the long procession moved on, rose up the chant of men's voices as it trailed onward, until the cemetery was reached.

Here, amid flowers and trees, was the open grave ; and as the priest's voice rose in prayer as the coffin was borne to its side, the metallic word of command to the soldiery, who had to return at once, clanged harshly ; but their heavy tramp soon ceased, and all was silent, save the priest's voice and the sobs of the mourners ; the four girls no more erect, but leaning one on the other in bitter sorrow, and as the coffin sank into the grave, there burst from one the bitter cry, 'Oh, Toni, Toni!' Whether he that was now laid in the earth was husband, brother, or betrothed, we knew not ; but this cry made us feel their grief was too sacred for strangers to be halting near. We moved from the scene of mourners and officers, with here and there the bright head-dress of a peasant, and we passed aside amid the trees ; noting here also, how very few were the trinkets and gewgaws on the tombs. Only natural flowers to ornament, and bespeak affection for those buried beneath.

Pilsen has always suffered terribly in the wars which have devastated Bohemia. Zizka made it his first stronghold, until Tabor was built, then the Papal party regained it and held it. In 1618 it was captured by Mansfeld, and in 1639 and 1648 it was twice besieged by the Swedes, but unsuccessfully ; and in the first Silesian War it was occupied by the French and Bavarians. In spite of all these destructive wars and sieges, Pilsen is now a most flourishing industrial town, with many manufactories and industries, and with an artisan population, eager to push forward the cause of higher wages and shorter hours of labour, their eagerness sometimes leading them to excesses; and once, on visiting the town, we found the factories guarded by armed soldiery, and heard the sad news that seventeen of the strikers had been shot in their attempt to seize a factory.

Very varied indeed are the works in Pilsen: steam-mills, tanneries, paper-works, machine factories, sawmills, etc.; but the all-important industry is that of brewing, for it is largely a communal matter, and the profits of the *Burgerliche Brauhaus*, or Town Brewery, that sends forth millions of gallons a year, are devoted to the good of the town: and to be a member of the Brewery Committee of the number of thirteen, is considered a very high honour in Pilsen. One peculiarity of this brewery is that they send forth nothing to anyone until they hold the actual cash for what is ordered. A visit to the quarter where stood all the great buildings and dwelling-houses connected with this brewery ended our visit to Pilsen, and then once more we travelled southwards to Budweis.

JAN'S COSTUME.
(From a drawing by H. Whatley.)

A MUSICIAN.

CHAPTER VIII.

FROM TABOR TO HOHENFURTH.

WE entered Budweis late at night, and the inn we had been recommended to we found large and rambling and vaulted as usual, but very dirty. An evening stroll seemed to promise us little; but in the cool morning we were early out in the great square, that covers an immense space of ground. The heavy old houses all round it are built over arches, thus forming a sheltered arcaded walk all round it, that is hung with goods of all descriptions. The great space was filled with marketers, and the deep, sonorous, rich-toned bells of a church hard by were tolling for prayers. Carts and yoked bullocks were mixed amid the marketers, that here were dressed in a deeper, richer, and more subdued scheme of colour than in Pilsen. Deep reds, and chocolates, and olive greens predominated; and as we watched the shifting colours, and remembered those of Pilsen, these of Budweis seemed to compare with the mellow rich tones of old stained cathedral glass, whilst Pilsen represented the brighter more vivid hues of modern stained glass.

The men wore round soft hats, jack-boots, and velvet vests with many buttons, and white shirts; these of course the richer peasants. The deep-toned bells lured us along beneath the arches to the church, the great square and domed tower of which rises high above the houses in one corner, whilst at the other side of the vast square are the triple onion-domed towers and gables of the town-hall. The church was crowded with women in dresses of deep red and brown, purple, black and dark orange, and deep blue, and dark green; their marketing *huttes* or baskets stood aside in nave and aisles, some filled with their heavy burdens, as the women kneel in prayer. Near the door was a fine handsome old man, with long white hair, and short jacket, velvet vest, and jack-boots; his head bent low in prayer. The men's side of the church was also very full, and when all issued forth, and we passed by the isolated tower out into the great square, the scene was full of beauty of soft, varied, subdued colour and life.

The marketers soon began to disperse (the traveller who 'lies a-bed a-mornings' will see none of these picturesque sights), and we bargained for a *Gelegenheit*, or carriage, to drive us out to the great modern castle, of Prince Schwarzenberg, of Frauenburg, as we were now within this overlord's district.

RAISING THE POLE ON MAY DAY.

We drove out into a wide plain across the Moldau, with a pretty retrospect of the town with its towers and bartizans, and around through various villages, strangely divided ; some being wholly German, others wholly Cech in population. We soon reached some big lakes, where flocks of birds, fish-divers, hovered over the reedy shores ; high hills rose away in the distance, and very quickly away on the right, on a dark wooded spur of the mountains, rose up the stately white buildings and towers of Frauenburg, the greatest modern castle in all Bohemia. As we drove on, we passed groups of gipsies with their waggons, and their women in deep tones of blue, red, and brown. At one encampment a child was laid in a basket, and a woman with a baby was guarding some goats beneath a knot of pines, and at a little distance was a group of women at work in the fields, in the favourite local tone of varied colours.

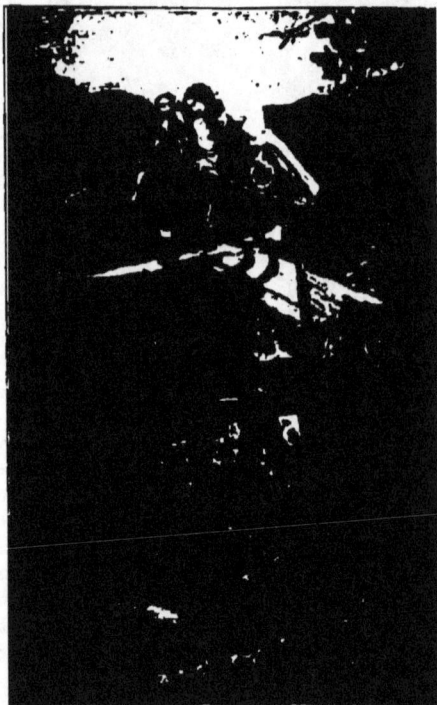

We turned aside ere ascending to the new castle, to visit the old hunting castle, up through lines of dark firs and light birches, past another lake with swans floating on it, and up a fine avenue of elms to the Jacobean château, surrounding a great square courtyard. We knew not what we w e r e to see, but here was another of our Bohemian surprises. We soon found we were in a most perfect forestry exhibition of a unique description. In the courtyard were sections of giant pines 295 and 450 years old, and as we entered the house, most varied

BOHEMIAN GIPSIES.

were the exhibits ; and every bird, animal, fish, reptile, and insect, and every tree, plant, egg to be found in the Schwarzenberg territory. Stags, eagles, boars, waterfowl, divers, storks, locusts, beetles, butterflies, all classed and arranged from the egg to full growth, or from baby animal to grandest example of full strength. All the furniture was of built-up forestry. Candelabra of horns and tusks, chairs and lounges and tables of skins and claws. Examples of all the woods, including those used for resonant instruments,

I

violins, guitars, etc. Strange examples of abnormal animals, every species of what an English hunter styles vermin. Enormous and most exact geological books of the century. Collections of the minerals and early implements of the stone and bronze ages, and some fine examples of early pottery ; one great urn of black ware eighteen inches across. In fact, so much was there to delight in and to study here, that we regretted we had not given a whole day to the Jagdschloss.. The castellan showed us with pride the last bear shot in the Böhmerwald on November 14, 1857. But the educational value of such a collection is beyond calculation, so scientifically, yet so charmingly and artistically and amusingly arranged, for the comic element was not omitted. But we had to leave it, and drive on past the lake to the great buildings of Frauenburg at the village of Podhrad. We soon entered the great courtyard of Frauenburg Castle, and began the survey of its treasures. Hall succeeded hall, and the woodwork, all of which was carved in the village beneath, was very fine and artistic. The general architecture is Tudor, combined with flamboyant, and the pictures, arms, trophies of the chase, and tapestry, and antiquities, make the time spent in passing through the halls go swiftly.

On leaving the castle, just as we reached our inn, a storm broke, and from the inn door we watched the vivid darting lightning flash out from the inky clouds, and strike as it were for. church and castle ; a brilliant though terrific sight, and then the rain descended in floods. In this district, and especially in the Bohemian mountains, these thunderstorms and floods are most frequent, regularly day after day at midday they burst on the traveller, and nought can withstand the drenching torrent of water.

In spite of the fact that our destination is now the famous town of Tabor, there is one church that should not be left unvisited in Budweis, if only the cloisters connected with it are seen, that is the church of the Virgin, now the Piaristenkloster. The windows are rich flamboyant, and fine pillars and vaulting are well preserved ; and some of the pictures still here are of interest ; and not far from it, close to the Rathhaus, is the museum, where the ethnologist and archæologist and historian will find much to perfect their education.

When we came out of this building, where we had been looking at the dresses of gold and silver of past Bohemians, we saw groups of pilgrims passing across the great square, all in a blaze of colour, being led by an old man who bore a cross, and another who played on a violin a strange plaintive chant, all with bent bodies, their bundles on their backs ; chanting as they went, they passed onwards to a famous pilgrimage church not far from the town.

In Bohemia the past life of Europe may still be studied in her villages and streets, even as in her museums ; pictures of life swiftly change ; and quickly after watching this mediæval scene we were in a train being borne on to that town about which we had read so much, the fortress from whence

sallied forth in their waggon forts the Hussites under their fierce blind leader
Zizka, the holy town of Tabor above Jordan's stream.   Tabor can also be
comfortably reached from Prague, and then a carriage can be taken, driving
through Bechza to Budweis.

We reached Tabor at nightfall, but early the next morning entered the
narrow streets lined with spring-
ing arches and quaint gables of
houses, up between which we
passed into the Ring ; and here
the first s i g h t of this most
curiously p i c t u r e s q u e space
enforced a halt.   It is in its
irregular a r c h i t e c t u r e and
strangeness unlike any other
square, and the first sight of it
is most impressive.

On one side of the square
rose the tall solid square tower,
with its curious high - peaked
roof, above the strangely gabled
Rathhaus and fantastically ornamented g a b l e s of the lower
houses.   Some more m o d e r n
houses intervened, with great
porte cochères and arched vault-
ings, but enough of the older
houses were left with the tall
triple-gabled Rathhaus to give
an excellent idea of this town
centuries ago, when this Ring-
platz was filled with armed men
under Zizka the victorious.   A
monument to the blind leader
now stands on the slope of the
place.   His helmet on his bent
head, with heavy moustache, a
great fur coat with d o u b l e
sleeves wrapped round him, over
his plate armour a shirt of mail,

A WELL-TO-DO PEASANT.

a terrible morning star in his right hand, and a great sword in his left.   An
effective and ably designed monument.

This town was built in the year 1420; it had no gradual beginning like
most towns, but sprang at once into an important place.   To this high rock

plateau, where once had stood an old castle, hurried a troop of Hussites under Hromadka, a bellfounder, who had just captured Austie from Ulrich of Austie, but who deemed this rocky height a safer fortress than Austie. Having gained possession of it, he sent off to Zizka, pointing out the advantages of the position ; and Zizka at once sent off from Pilsen a knight with a troop of proved warriors to hold it and to fortify it ; and thus was founded this famous town of Tabor.

The immense power that its inhabitants wielded throughout the mighty

TABOR.   [*From an Old Print.*

struggle against the Papal power, is an example of what intense enthusiasm will effect against tremendous odds, and the history of the Taborites is full of exciting episodes.

Around this rocky height on one side was the lake, on the other side was the river Lusinitz ; and connecting river and lake was a smaller stream, and with the exception of the sloping road that now runs out to the railway road, the town was perched on a precipitous rock, with water at its base. The old walls, and bastions, and towers still run round the town, and alternate with the houses that here and there were tree-sheltered. At one level spot on the walls, overlooking the waterfalls, where the brook joined the Jordan, we found a small cattle-market established; and oxen and hooded waggons and peasants in bright dresses all harmonised with towers and embattlements. Only the absence of armed men in helm and breastplate was wanting to carry us back to the fifteenth-century struggle.

The Taborites were the most advanced of the two sections into which the Hussites divided about 1420. They held strong Protestant views with regard to the chief doctrines and practices of the Romish Church. They accepted much of Wyclif's teaching, and were strengthened and supported in their determination by our countryman, Peter Payne, who joined the Taborites, as representing the purest of Wyclif's followers.

When first founded, there was no 'mine and thine' in Tabor; everything was in common, as with the Apostles, and the code of their teaching is very instructive.

Mass could be said in ordinary clothes, as the acolytes assert to this day, and no church was necessary; the consecrating words of Christ were to be used, and no others. Chapels and churches dedicated to special saints, setting God in the background, were to be considered as heathenish, and destroyed. Bones and remains of saints were not to be kept or worshipped. Purgatory was not to be believed in, or the dead to be prayed for. None were to bow before the Sacrament as before God, a practice they held to be idolatry. They maintained that no rite administered by a vicious priest was valid, that the service of the Church should be in the native language, and that pious laymen and even women were eligible to preach. Together with these religious decrees there was a curious admixture of the ideas that the Socialists of to-day promulgate: no king, no rulers, no taxes. Each for all and all for each, with God alone as King and Ruler.

In spite of this communistic and socialistic type of creed, the Taborites were obedient enough to their fierce leader Zizka, and the horrible cruelties practised against them, and their fierce retaliations, are an awful page in the long chapter of war in Religion's name by sects and churches.

At length we entered the town-hall, and, with the guidance of the courteous and helpful town-clerk, looked over the treasures preserved in the museum there. We saw many antiquities carefully preserved, that helped us to understand Tabor's former importance. One of the most interesting was the arms of the town carved in stone in the year 1515, embracing the double-headed black eagle with the two-tailed Bohemian lion in red, above the open gate of the town, and between two high-roofed towers. This is enclosed in a panel, carved, in which are woven branches, and 'mid the branches is modelled Jan Hus in flames, with the cap on his head; Jerome also in flames upon piled faggots; and below are figures of a naked man and a woman; and on the opposite side figures of Prokop, the great leader, and blind

Zizka.   The two nude figures represent members of the sect of the
Adamites, a strange outcome of these worried, harassed days.   They, somewhat
like the Positivists of to-day, declared there was neither God nor devil
beyond good and bad people.   Property was a crime; marriage was a sin;
everything must be in common; and as they were innocent, some went naked
as in Paradise.   These and worse excesses led to their utter annihilation
by Zizka, who preserved one only alive, that he might give an account of
their belief.   The history of the various sects of this period embodies a

From a drawing.   FOUNTAIN IN THE SQUARE AT TABOR.   *By Walter Crane.*

description of nearly every strange sect of tc-day, so little does human
nature change.

A Book of Trades of 1545 gave excellent pictures of the dresses of the
period.   Zizka's mail shirt is preserved here, and above it is his likeness,
painted in the later Jesuit period, giving him a Judas‧face.   Some of the
earliest Bohemian coins of 1109 are here, and tongs for baking the wafers
for the church.   A Cech Bible of 1488, and a Herrenhut Bible of 1585, the
latter as the Luther Bibles, with Luther on the cover.

A strange relic of past heathendom is seen in some eggs that were
built into a wall in 1420; the gradual descent from walling in a living

being, first a man, then a lamb, then a hen, and at last an egg, the germ of life only.

But this museum must hold us no longer, and forth from it we sallied to make the tour of the walls, now with a local professor, who spoke French, and the town clerk, who spoke German ; and as we walked on under and above the grey grim old walls, under strange towers and massive buildings, we looked out to the monastery of Klokot, where forty of the Adamites were burnt ; and to the Bechyn Gate, from whence is a lovely view of town and valley, and deep forest vale where the Adamites lived in their fancied Paradise.

The tower of Kotnov dates from 1232, before the founding of the town ; and the gate near it still has its pulleys and chains for drawbridge *in situ ;* and as we walk on, with items of history and folklore streaming into our ears on one side from the professor in French, and on the other side from the town-clerk in German, our English notes get mixed ; but we hear so much of strange spots and strange legends, all to be studied near and in Tabor, that a month will hardly suffice to see and study all.

There is the mediæval buried town of Pribenice, the rich monastery and pilgrimage resort of Bechyn, old Tabor, and the island Waly, where the Adamites made their last fierce

AN OLD HOUSE IN TABOR, SHOWING THE STONE COMMUNION TABLE.

stand ; and numberless villages and castles, where most gorgeous costumes on *fête* and pilgrimage days can be marvelled at ; and learning of all these, we re-entered the town, and stood once more in the Ring, and were shown how in former days the Taborites took the Communion in the open air, at stone tables in front of their houses in this square. Some twenty or thirty of these stone tables stood here then, and one of them still stands before a richly decorated house ; a strange silent witness of a most strange past.

Tabor and its surrounding country has an enticing fascination, and as its hotel is also most excellent, it is always revisited with pleasure. Space compels us to thus only hint at the strange spots clustering round it, for we must go south again, and re-enter Budweis, to explore that part of

Bohemia that lies near the southern boundary mountains, known as the Böhmerwald.

There are two ways of getting to Krumau by road. We chose the shortest route, as on this particular journey we wished to get early into Krumau to visit Prince Schwarzenberg's castle, and this caused us to omit the great ruin of Maidstein, that can easily be reached from the village of Opalic, with a lovely walk of an hour down the Moldau Valley to Goldenkron. Near this Maidstein is a great wall, dating back to the days of the Marcomen tribes; the present Maidstein ruin itself dates from 1349, and was so called because Jost I. of Rosenberg rebuilt the castle for the residence of his five maiden sisters, until they were married. Its destruction is due to the Swedes in the Thirty Years' War.

Only a word can be given to the Cistercian monastery at Goldenkron, although a chapter or two might be written upon it. It was founded in 1263, and called the Golden Crown, because it possessed a thorn said to have been taken from the Crown of Thorns. In 1420 the Hussites stormed it.

In Bohemia, if one ventures to leave the marked-out route, castle and village and monastery start up, or strange, seductive mountain scenery leads one on, and the original idea is lost in unthought-of and unheard-of wonders.

Our present route is through the village of Steinkirchen, past gipsy camps and over great tracks of hill-land and forest. As we passed through this village all the school-children were out on a green slope, the little crowd of girls in every bright colour by themselves, and the grey group of boys by themselves, who all raised their hats as we passed, the little girls making their *knicksen* (courtesy). At the village of Kossau was a pretty scene of a lake bordered with green slopes and dark pines, and we then wound up to a high plateau that was alternated with pine forests and cultivated farms with game in plenty. In one spot here we saw a woman mending the roads, clad in a bright red dress to the knees, below which appeared her bare brown legs. She wore a black silk jacket, and a light pink apron, and a dark stuff headdress, a most picturesque figure on the roadside. After the village of Rojau we crossed the swift-flowing, clear Moldau, and joined here the route from Goldenkron. Some of the teams of horses on this route were decked most picturesquely with long brass trappings, hung with green and red; and at the toll gates the collectors were interesting; one pretty girl, in the usual bright colours and red stockings, spoke German. We thought of that Duke of Austria who preferred a toll-gate keeper's pretty daughter to the court ladies.

Soon after leaving Rojau we crossed over a high plain, and beneath us in a deep valley were the towers of Krumau. Down the hillside we drove, between firs and rocks, and soft green meadows at their feet, with piles of sweet-scented timber for the rafts by the river's side, a most lovely entrance into the town along by the swift-flowing river, with before us the old gabled houses, and above the great castle with spires and towers and minarets. Then over a wooden bridge, with the bubbling, leaping river beneath us, teams of horses in brilliant trappings, and slow, patient oxen in the bullock-waggons, and ahead the old gate tower of the town, its high-peaked roof falling into harmony with the castle's towers. Under its narrow archway we drove, and on into the inn yard just ahead of it, where we were welcomed by the host and led through the bright kitchens of the inn into the guest-chamber.

PRINCE SCHWARZENBERG'S ARMY.

Crossing over the drawbridge we looked down upon a bear-pit, and then entered the courtyard, which is painted with frescoes, and in which stands a sentry, and the guard in the famous blue and white uniform of the Schwarzenbergers. This prince is the only one in Austria allowed to have an army and a uniform of his own. In their hats they wear cocks' feathers, and as they strolled back and forward before their cannon, looked somewhat conscious of being but play soldiers. Like the Prince of Monaco's army, Prince Schwarzenberg's is small, numbering thirty-two men.

This castle is one of the best preserved in Bohemia, and, like Friedland, has the old and the new blended in a picturesque mass of irregular building. We had been for some time in the country of the Schwarzenbergs, and now we were in the house of the Rosenbergs, the powerful family that for centuries held sway in Bohemia. Ulrich of Rosenberg being the Warwick, the king-maker of the Hussite period, sided at one time with Sigmund, at others with the Utraquists or Chalicers, who demanded to have both the bread and the wine in the Communion. In 1420 he leaned to Sigmund's side and encamped against Tabor, and vowed to take the Sacrament of bread only, to which act the Taborites responded, 'They knew he was a cripple in body, and now they knew he was a cripple in soul.' A certain Niklas of Hus fell on his camp simultaneously with the Taborites, and defeated him so fearfully, though one against twenty, that camp and treasure, gold and silver, were left behind, and guns, and slings, and catapults, which defeat sent Ulrich into such a passion that he at once imprisoned all the Utraquist priests in his castles of Pribein, Chustnik, Helfenburg, Krumau, Rosenberg, and Gratzen, tortured them, and left them in the Hunger towers until some died. This happened in June. In November he lost Prachatic, a town we shall soon visit, and then he began to parley with the Taborites ; and in April 1421, when even the mighty Lord Cenek of Wartenberg was on his knees to the Prague warriors, Ulrich announced that King Sigmund agreed to the Prague Articles. In 1426 he writes : He 'could not hang the Hussites openly as before, they were too powerful; but when they caught them they drowned them, or tortured them to death secretly,' and at the same moment he held a council with the Taborites, and made a truce with them. But Ulrich, the principal agent of Emperor Sigmund, the 'richest and most cunning of the Bohemian nobles,' could not suppress Hus's followers. He afterwards bore a most important part in the crowning of King Albert, and then joined with the barons against the royal party ; and again shifted to the king's side when King Ladislaus was born. It was from Krumau, where we stand, that he aided the monk Capistran to go forth and preach against George of Podiebrad ; and in 1452, in this castle, in Capistran's presence, after thirty years' fruitless struggles against the Hussites, he abjured worldly matters, handed over the rule of the Rosenberg house to his son, and spent ten years between this castle and that of Maidstein, and died April 28, 1462.

Such a glimpse into the life of a great baron of Bohemia in the Middle Ages makes one understand the life and scenes that these castles, with dungeons and halls, chapels and battlements, have witnessed ; and after this glimpse into human life of the past we enter the chapel. The arms of the various branches of these families and their genealogical tree can be studied on the walls; but the beauty of the castle lies in its position, and from a balcony is a most lovely view of all its towers and arcades and minarets, and bronze domes and spires, with the river below and the clustering houses on the left hand; and on the right the brown Moldau flowing in amber tints over a weir, lashed in yellow foam and shadowed by high wooded hills.

The picture galleries are very long, and contain some curious but not many good pictures. One called the 'Taking of Troy' is an excellent representation of a mediæval town. A great gallery leads to the gardens over a bridge, beneath which rushed a lovely mass of tawny flood water; from one of the picture galleries we watched the long rafts shooting the rapids of the Moldau, and it was exciting to see the handy manipulation of these apparently unwieldy snakes of timber, directed with the great sweeps into the exact space of the fall; the leap of the rowers on to the high seats, as they swept into the surging water, and the great lengths of tied timbers swept down the foaming torrent, swung round to a nicety into the narrow sluice falls; and above and around were the peaked hills and the fields, and the clustering buildings of the old castle.

The archives of Krumau are priceless, and the archives, documents, and manuscripts of the Rosenbergs are continually referred to by Palacky, who writes history solely, where possible, from original letters and contemporary writings.

A RAFTSMAN AT KRUMAU.

The town of Krumau is extremely picturesque, the life of past ages and of to-day blended pleasantly; and as we wandered about it we got wondrous peeps between its steep narrow streets of the mighty castle with its great tower. This has a solid Norman-like base, with Romanesque windows leading up to an arcaded balcony with bronze pents, and above this a gabled storey with bronze roofs and spires, surmounted by gold balls; and this again topped by an open belfry with similar bronze roofs and spire and golden balls, and capped by a spike with a banneret.

After studying this, it was pleasant to stroll out to the bridge and watch the peasantry coming in over the bridge to mass, for it was a *fête*

day. In under the arch of the high-peaked tower gate they streamed, the
book of the mass in their hands, or with their baskets of ware in all
colours. As we watched we saw dresses of pink, red, blue, black, green,
orange, brown, mauve, violet, stream in, and the wearers cross themselves
before St. John of Nepomuc; and yet the population of the town is largely
German, and we heard the complaint that Prince Schwarzenberg was striving
to Bohemianise them.

We drove out of Krumau upon the opposite side to which we had
entered it, with most artistic peeps back at the clustering town over a
great weir with tawny, silvery, foaming water rushing over it; then over
another bridge, and we were in the country, but meeting crowds of peasants
in all colours, with their bullock waggons pressing in to the *fête;* rafts
were shooting the falls of the river beneath, and the whole scene was
romantic and very full of life and colour and beauty.

Yet a third bridge we had to cross, and we were in the midst of
lovely scenery, trees and meadows and rocks alternating around us. We
had kept to our coachman from Budweis, and to disprove the absurd
stories of extortionate charges in Bohemia, we may mention that the charge
each day for this carriage and pair, including all fees, which are unknown
in fact, was six gulden a day, that is, twelve francs, or barely ten
shillings.

The drive we now had before us was to visit the Castle of Rosenberg, and
then some miles beyond the renowned Cistercian monastery of Hohenfurth.
A charming succession of scenes opened up as we drove on; here were
women in bright groups washing their clothes in the river, then black
smoke arose in the valley, and we passed a cellosen factory; we also saw
the glazed black-faced men returning from the graphite pits. Ever onward
by the Moldau we drove, rustic wooden trestle bridges crossed it here and
there; in one spot we looked down upon four bends of the bright stream.
There hung a soft haze over the scene, and in the distance the river was
of a soft dark blue tone. Here we were high above it, but soon again we
were on its level by its banks, and we saw a gipsy encampment, with its
occupants making their morning toilet. An old man was shaving in front
of the low tents, a woman was combing her long dark hair, a brown-
bodied naked little child was running about, whilst another woman was
nursing a red swathed baby, another naked child having a morning wash
in the stream. Shortly after by the roadside we passed a shepherd lad
winding off on two sticks his wool for knitting, whilst not far from this lad
by the roadside we saw still lying in his morning sleep an old grey-
bearded Bohemian, his wife being occupied in gathering sticks for the
morning fire. Scene succeeded scene of nomad life or pastoral activity,
forming vignettes of artistic sketches, as when we saw a young girl in
pink head-gear and pink dress pick up the little black kid of a black goat

that followed her caressingly ; or a group of wandering apprentices passed
with bundles and boots on their backs. But such scenes were soon
succeeded by a grand avenue of beech-trees, then a lovely bit of road
beside the foaming river, a brilliant kingfisher on a rock was undisturbed
by our wheels : on through the lovely country we went, until high on a hill

THE CASTLE OF ROSENBERG.

we saw a round tower, then below two other towers with a great wandering
castle beneath them ; a high wooden bridge on stone pillars spanned two
hills, and across this we went, and round a curious tongue of precipitous
rock, on which was perched the Castle of Rosenberg, a truly romantic
situation.   Down round the rock tongue we wound, and as we turned it we
met the people coming from the church, a fine Decorated building ; and
before the church were the old fire-engines, decorated with flowers, and
we then found it was St. Florian's Day, the saint who protects from fire,

and from the look of the engines it was better to trust to St. Florian than to the engines for aid in need. We pulled up at the Gasthaus, and found it filled with peasants in round velvet hats with small silver buckles, short round jackets, and velvet vests; and as we entered the priest in black and white robes came in, and all hats were doffed. We could not linger here, however picturesque was the scene, but climbed up to the castle. Over the entrance were some bears' heads and skulls, the last killed in the neighbourhood, and we found the castle divided into new and old parts, the old only going back to the sixteenth century; but a round tower with dungeons beneath, standing in a garden between the two buildings, is probably of thirteenth-century origin.

Long could we have strayed amid all the choice and deeply interesting antiquities preserved here. Armour and instruments of torture in one hall, one curious item being a thief's mask; the tongue was made to protrude, and then a needle was pierced through it. In another room were the most delicate examples of Venetian and Bohemian glass, and our guide kindly played upon some of these, the tone from them being as of a soft pure-toned horn. Silk needlework, crystal, ivory, and pearl-handled forks, inlaid and minutely carved. Silver and gold beaten caskets, illuminated psalters, inlaid tables, portraits of the possessors of the castle, and curious religious pictures. The Lords of Rosenberg, whose arms bear the rose somewhat as our Tudor rose, became extinct after Peter Vok, whose portrait is preserved here; from him it descended to his sister Eva's son, Johann v. Zriny, and from him it came into the hands of the Schwambergs, who lost it after the battle of the White Mountain at Prague, for Ferdinand II. confiscated it, and gave it to Count Buguoz, in whose family it still remains. Of course there is a legend connected with the castle; all these castles have their legends, some examples we must give ere we close this volume.

Astonished at all the art-treasures we were looking upon, we turned the visitors' book back for some years to try and find an English name, but finding none we turned to our guide and asked her if she ever had any English visitors, as on our entry she had asked what countrymen we were. Her answer was emphatic and prompt: '*Niemals! niemals!*' Never! never! Had not this been our common experience we should have been more surprised; but as we looked round now at the charming hall, and out of the windows on to the delicious views, we felt regret almost that our countrymen (at least, some of them) had never been here.

Our long and exciting morning reminded us at length we had ordered lunch; and at the inn we found the inevitable Schnitzel and potatoes, followed by an excellent omelette and capital wine and bread, and our bill, including the coachman's and horses' dinner, that is, for five men and two horses, came to 2·56, equal to five francs, or say four shillings; and we found that carriages here could be obtained at rather less rates than we were paying.

On leaving Rosenberg we wound up above a great fir forest to a plateau of green cornfields; on through villages we went, but soon from a plain we saw ahead the spires of Hohenfurth, and then the immense square monastery with its slight spired church rising above it. We were disappointed as we drove through the long village, for all the buildings of the

THE CHAPTER-HOUSE, HOHENFURTH.

monastery seemed new; but we withheld our decision. Right well we knew how pleasantly Bohemia could disappoint us. Upon entering the monastery we were taken in charge by a young brother in his white robe; and under his guidance we were quietly and leisurely led through cloisters and chapter-house and the various halls of the monastery.

The church, which we first visited, we found to be of good Decorated architecture, but somewhat thin in material; the stalls and confessionals were all of inlaid wood. The apse was wholly hid by a great gilt altar-piece. The cloisters were good Decorated work dating from the fourteenth century. Within the monastery the halls were illustrated by paintings; two of Peter Boch, or Vok of Rosenberg, the founder of the house; one depicting his being saved from the *hohen-fluth* (high flood), and the other his giving the church, were especially of interest. This happened in 1250. The chapter-house dates from 1529, and is a good example of architecture of that date, supported by a central pillar from which the vaulting radiates. A very beautiful rose window highly decorated is in this chapter-house.

From the church we were taken into the famous library, and were told of the historic archives that are preserved here. Palacky makes good and frequent use of these. Alas, that so many rich and choice historic documents were destroyed, when the storm of rage and revenge burst over Bohemia after the White Mountain defeat at Prague! Then, in 1621, fierce laws were enacted which made it impossible for one not a Romanist to live in Bohemia; and the poorer people were cut to pieces, broken on the wheel, hung, beheaded, branded with hot irons on the forehead, or deprived of their noses or ears, whilst the Jesuits traversed the country, with soldiers to protect them, to carry out the decrees. Thousands then fled into the forests, and still retained the Hussite faith; and this accounts for the Bohemian love for forest praying-places unconsecrated by the Church. But after 1627 the population of Bohemia sank by banishment or death from four millions to eight hundred thousand souls; and at this period thousands of the most precious manuscripts were also destroyed by the Jesuits, whose name is ever execrated in Bohemia by the people, be they Romanist or Protestant, as we have seen. But in spite of all ravages of man and time, Hohenfurth possesses one hundred and fifty volumes of parchment MSS., and about a thousand volumes of paper MSS., and some forty thousand volumes of books; a rich mine, much of which is still to be explored. In the library we also saw clever pen-and-ink sketches by the brothers, and amongst other treasures shown were the Lord's Prayer written in a hundred tongues, their oldest book, dated 1469, a fine Psalter of the fourteenth century, etc. In the theological hall the picture on the ceiling is of Christ in the Temple. The picture hall is a good Romanesque hall of three aisles, divided by two lines of pillars. Amongst the pictures are some by Titian, and here was shown us a book annotated by Melanchthon, and a chain scourge that must have inflicted horrible torture.

Whilst here one of our party sneezed, and it was curious to note the courtly bow of the brother, his equivalent of the *Wohlsein* of the peasant, to exorcise the devil within one, even as our 'God bless you!' still lingers and is now and then heard in England.

In the hall of antiquities were many treasures, and in one little hall

were Dutch and other paintings. 'Every house is said to have a skeleton
in it,' said the brother, as he stood in his long white robe by an upright
cupboard ; suddenly he threw open a narrow door, and there stood a white
polished skeleton of a miller lad who had been hung for some offence. He
also showed us some leather made from the miller-lad's skin, a good
collection of minerals, and the last banners presented by the Rosenbergs, a
sand clock, a curious old Dutch altar of the birth of Christ, and far more
interesting objects than can be mentioned here.

When we were asked to place our names in the book of the monastery
we again looked over it and asked our usual question, if they had ever had
any English here, but the answer came, 'No, never,' as we were now
accustomed to expect.

Once more we drove on away from deeply interesting Hohenfurth.
After a long, steep ascent we reached the little station of Zartlesdorf, and
dismissed our good friend the coachman. Here on this height was no sign
of budding spring, no burst in the hawthorn hedge even; but that night we
were at lovely Linz on the Danube, amid the shady, full-flowering chestnut
trees, and in hot summer; but Linz is not in Bohemia, and we must
retrace our steps once more to Budweis, for yet another drive of equally
surprising interest.

From a drawing]   CHODEN COSTUME.   *[by H. Whatley.*

K

From a drawing]   BOHEMIAN TINKER.   [by Walter Crane.

CHAPTER IX.

Prachatic and the Birthplace of Hus.

IT was upon a hot afternoon in May that once again we found ourselves driving out of Budweis, this time westwards instead of southwards, towards Prachatic or Prachatitz. As evening drew on we passed through a rich fruit country, and at last in a low valley we saw the brown towers and embattled walls with the clustered houses of Prachatic; and above houses and walls the excessively high-roofed church, with its picturesque domed campanile. How strange was our entry into it under embattled gateways, and resonant archways, into the picturesque sgraffitoed square !

We had not been long in the inn, a most comfortable old hostelry, named after Prince Rudolf, but dating back in the centuries, ere the

From a drawing]   THE BLACK TOWER AND RING, KLATTAU.   [by H. Whatley.

Dean of Prachatic, to whom our letters introduced us, entered ; and under his guidance on the morrow we explored the town, still encircled by walls and towers, and with many of its houses still illuminated by sgraffito illustrations of scriptural, allegorical, and philosophical subjects.

To describe Prachatic thoroughly would take up far more space than we are allowed. In spite of plague, and fire, and war, the town preserves much of its mediævalism ; and being nearly twenty English miles from a railway, its present life is of the age before steam. The watchman patrols the streets and calls the hours ; the busy shuttle of the hand-loom weaver is heard rattling in the small but busy factories. The diligence or post waggon comes rattling in with blast of horn over the stony street, underneath the embattled town gates, on which, in bright colours, is a great fresco of William of Rosenberg on horseback, with sententious mottoes and the arms of this once powerful family.

A proof of the antiquity and importance of the town is obtained in the fact, that in the eleventh century King Wratislas gave the town and its tolls to the Chapter of the Wysehrad. These tolls were exceedingly rich. Bohemia has no salt in its borders, and most of the salt passed over the Bohemian mountains and by Prachatic, and an illustration of the fertility and industry of the Bohemians in the fifteenth century is afforded us by the fact that Pope and Kaiser were unable to establish a salt blockade and famine, because the neighbouring lands must purchase the rich products of Bohemia, and they paid for them in salt. In the fourteenth century the school of Prachatic was of known importance. The famous Christian of Prachatic studied here, and, it is suggested, Hus and Zizka ; a suggestion not without probability, as it was the nearest school to Hus's birthplace. The illustration standing as frontispiece shows it much as it is now. There is the great square gate with its forework, and its double arches and embattle-ments, still with some cannon-balls embedded in it ; and its pulleys for drawbridge and portcullis in position. There is the inner higher second tower, and the embattled houses leading round to the great church. All still adorned with the frescoes of former days, faint now, but discernible. The great church door has been patched inside, but outside are the marks of axes and hammers and bullet-holes of the storming in the year 1620. The rich stone-work around it is still full of beauty. Inside the church is very rich in Renaissance, and echoes of a still echoing fierce past. Quaint pictures and statuary, and wood carvings on stalls and seat ends, with quaint mottoes, demand and gain interested attention ; and outside on the walls of the new deanery, where our good friend the dean showed us some rich missals and old Bibles, and also on the outer walls of the church, are some most expressive and quaint frescoes of scriptural and other subjects.

The town hall is richly decorated with frescoes, and so are many of the other arcaded houses, some still having the old, now faint, work of past centuries, others with the colours renewed, but the old work copied, some, unfortunately, harshly and glaringly repeated. The square in which it stands has suffered terribly from siege and fire; the marvel is that aught is left of the past. Zizka early in his career took possession of the town, but on his quitting it some retaliation was taken on the Hussites by the Catholics, a priest and one or two burgers being burnt in the square; and Zizka returned, and in forcible language demanded the gates to be opened; but the Catholics laughed at him. The fierce Taborists under Zizka soon stormed the walls, drove off the defenders or slew them with their terrible flails, and took the town; they killed or took prisoners all the men. Zizka acknowledged seven

A BOHEMIAN PRAYING SERVICE.

as good Hussites; eighty-five he shut up in the sacristy of the church, piled up pitch and straw around it and about them, and so burnt them. This fashion of shutting up your enemies in a crowd in a hut or building and burning them to death was a favourite one on both sides in this terrible blood struggle; fierce cruel deeds on the one side were revenged by crueller, if possible, deeds on the other. If the Hussites burnt one priest, the Catholics burnt two, or *vice versâ*. After the appeal to arms Christian teaching was often ignored. The old sacristy is still shown, and the bent bars of the high windows are said to be those bent by these poor victims of sectarian hatred, but this is doubtful.

We witnessed late one evening, just outside the great gate of the town, an instance of how the right and freedom to worship God without the aid of priest still clings to the Bohemian. Here there is a little chapel or shrine, and in and around it, lit up by candles, was a most pathetic and picturesque group of peasants. Men, women, and children were on their knees, an old grey-haired man was in the centre, he reciting the prayers and leading the hymns, and all around him were the older women, with an outside ring of children. No priest was near; and this type of service is a very common one with the Bohemian peasantry.

Much of the walls and moat and many of the towers are still extant round the town ; and the walks and excursions round it are very pleasant ; and should the town life of Prachatic be too exciting (to a lover of history and antiquity it is exciting), the overwrought citizen can walk out to the great forests of the Böhmerwald. On the edge of the pines, with sombre, silent walks, is a little bath establishment called the Margarethenbad, where he can have forest silence or Bohemian society chatter ; for this bath is much frequented in summer, but needless to say no English are to be met there.

We drive out of Prachatic over drawbridge and under archways on to the Netolic road, soon to bear away to the left, and on towards the birth-place of him whose soul went out in flames at Constance, that mighty Bohemian reformer, Jan Hus. We were eager to look upon the village where more than five centuries ago was born in low estate the man whose name still resounds through the world, and is upon every man's tongue in Bohemia, be he Romanist or Protestant. Soon after leaving the Netolic road, the view opens out of a fine range of hills, encircling a rich plain, in the middle of which is the small town of Husinec, lying in a deep green-sloped valley. The light-brown, square church tower, with grey onion-domed cap, rises above the deep red brown roof of the church, and the white clustering and red roofs of the solid square houses. The low, level rich fields are dotted with cattle, brightly dressed women and boys guarding them. The little river Blanitz goes rippling and gurgling onwards, and in the light of the morning sun larks rise up from the meadows, and join their outburst of song to the twitter of other birds.

The high hills beyond are capped with pines, whose young shoots on the lower slopes are bright and freshly green. A flock of divers rise from the river's bank, as our approach alarms them ; the hot sun pours down on us fiercely, but the soft green valley is full of peace ; it seems shut in by rising mountain and hill from all echoes of the world's strife ; and only the river and the gull-like birds speak of the outer world and the sea, from whence came the words from Wyclif's lips that echoed into this quiet vale, and from here re-echoed back throughout the world, teaching the right of each man's soul to appeal direct to God the Creator, with no human intervention.

As we enter the village between lines of fruit-trees, the river has worn a deep bed between black rocks that come out from the sloping green hillside ; and now across the stream we go upon a wooden trestle bridge ; women are washing their clothes in the river, and the pink bedding is airing beneath the trees. As we stroll up between the houses, some of the square solid stone type, others of brown timber with wooden galleries, we see in a niche of the Decorated order, a figure of a saint wearing a biretta,

From a drawing]   [*by Walter Crane.*

PEASANTS PRAYING BEFORE A STATUE OF JOHN HUS, ALTERED TO JOHN OF NEPOMUC.

with the five-starred halo round his head. St. John of Nepomuc now, but the thin white face, with beard and moustache, is surely the face of John Hus. It is exactly the same as Hus is represented in the great picture by Broznik of 'Hus before the Council at Constance,' and as he is represented upon contemporary seals and paintings. Is this one of the cases which we were assured by our artist friend at Turnau were numerous, where the statue of the *heilige Jan Hus* had been modified into the *heilige Jan Nepomuc?* These statues are constantly used by the peasantry as praying places.

But we stayed our conjectures and entered the church. It was decorated for a *fête*, with trees and bannerets by the side of the altar; but with the exception of a holy-water font all was new and restored. Outside the church on a high mound at three cross-roads is a well, and from here we looked down on a strange scene. A group of men, women, and children were singing in good harmony, whilst not far off, under an arch leading into a farm, stood a coffin with priests and acolytes and women around it, 'the boys bearing lighted tapers, and standing partly in the gloom of the dark archway, where the daily work went on, though one lay silent in the black coffin on the threshold.

We posted a letter in Husinec, and found the post-office to be an old solid arched room with the post-mistress's bed in it; and at the little inn we noted the violin and flute lying on the table. The group of singers we had noted also carried instruments, so that the love of music is not absent in Husinec. Down a very wide long street we passed, the solid houses having great arched doors, outside which were stretched bright red and blue stockings that had been dyed, for the villagers are a busy people, wool-spinners and stocking-weavers, fez-makers, and match-makers. It is curious to think that the Turks, who once nearly swept and conquered the whole of this district, should now get their head-gear from these Bohemians; but our thoughts on this were cut short by seeing on our right hand a bronze medallion upon a cottage wall. We were before the birthplace of John Hus.

The old house was of the square solid order that could withstand the wear of centuries. Five stone steps led up to a door, now partially walled in and closed with shutters. By the side of the steps, low down, was another arched door, and over this was a little inscription: 'Mistr Jan Hus dur 8 Cervne, 1369,' and above this a good bronze medallion of Hus's thin face and somewhat pointed beard, the hair long, and the sharp, clear, intellectual features in good relief. Inside the house the steps down show there was a room below where the steps go up outside. In the room where Hus was born are now hung on the walls wreaths and mottoes borne here by his patriotic countrymen; there is a copy of Broznik's picture of Hus before the Council, a little cupboard all worn and cut away, and the old worm-eaten planks bespeak great age. A visitors' book is kept here, but few are the names except those of Bohemians and Germans. A line of music in it caught our eyes:

and attached to these seven bars of music was the now famous signature of Antonin Dvořak, the great musical composer. We could see no English name in the book, and the good dame at the cottage expressed surprise when we told her we were English. It seemed strange to us as

Englishmen, free from the thraldom of a foreign ecclesiastical power, and from the superstitions of a corrupt Church ; free from priestcraft largely through the teaching of our countrymen, John Wyclif and William Tindale, to stand in this little house. Here was born in 1369 the noble martyr Jan Hus, who loved the Word of God, and preached it to his countrymen, and who helped to spread through Europe Wyclif's teaching.   Strange indeed to stand in this birthroom of Hus, thankful for his help, after having just looked upon the statue of his supplanter in Bohemia, Jan of Nepomuc, and witnessed in Hus's village a funeral with the rites of Rome, but

THE HOUSE IN WHICH JOHN HUS WAS BORN AT HUSINEC.

now of tolerant Rome, for Hus still speaks with a mighty voice in Bohemia.

Of the early life of John Hus nothing is known, save that he was educated first in Husinec and Prachatic, and then at the University of Prague, where he graduated B.A. 1393, B.D. 1394, and M.A. 1396.   In 1402 he was made rector or curate of the Bethlehem Chapel at Prague, and began that popular preaching which stirred the heart of the nation, which developed his own religious life, and which became the moving force in the Bohemian Reformation.   We have no space here to describe the great movement.   Hus accepted much of Wyclif's teaching, both as regards the Church and Scripture, and defended and taught it in Prague.   The bull of

Pope Alexander V. condemning these views was published in Prague in 1410, and a number of Wyclif's books were publicly burnt. This caused the controversy between the followers of Hus and the Papal adherents to rage more fiercely than ever, and in 1414 the Council of Constance was summoned. Though Hus was induced to go there under the 'safe conduct' of the Emperor Sigismund, he was thrown into prison, denied a trial, and treacherously martyred July 6, 1415, in the forty-sixth year of his age. Some of his correspondence has come down to us, and we quote a few extracts from one of his letters, to show what manner of man he was, and what manner of teaching pope, emperor, and priest combined to crush. About the time when Wyclif's books were burnt, Richard Fitz, one of Wyclif's English helpers and friends, wrote to Hus to encourage him in the stand he was making on behalf of Wyclif's views. The following passage is from a letter written by Hus as a reply to the one which Richard Fitz had sent to him :—

'John Hus to Master Richard, England, 1410.—Dearly beloved in Christ Jesus, may the peace of Christ reign in your hearts through the Holy Spirit which is given unto you. Your loving letter, which has come down to me from the Father of Lights, has powerfully moved the hearts of the brethren in Christ, for it contained in it so much tenderness, resolution, strength, and consolation, that if antichrist had succeeded in swallowing up every other writing of the kind in the jaws of hell, it by itself would have sufficed for believing Christians to their salvation. Therefore I, pondering over in my mind its substance and its strength, said to the multitude in my public preaching, at which I estimate almost 10,000 people were present, " Look, beloved brethren, what great interest the most faithful preachers of Christ in foreign lands have in your salvation, in that they desire to pour out their whole heart if only they may keep us in the law of the Lord." And I added, "See, our dearly beloved Richard, the helper of Master John Wyclif in the matters of the Gospel, has written you such an encouraging letter, that if I had no other, I should feel encouraged to give up even my life for the Gospel of Christ, and this will I do by the help of our Lord Jesus Christ." The faithful in Christ were so inflamed with zeal by your letter, that they entreated me to translate it into our native language.

'Know, dearest brother, that the people wish to hear nothing save the Holy Scripture, especially the Gospel and Epistles, and wherever, in town or country, in court or castle, a preacher of the holy truth shows himself, people run there in crowds, neglecting the clergy of irregular lives. And the consequence of this is, that Satan has aroused himself because the tail of Behemoth has been touched, and it remains for Jesus Christ to crush his head. I myself have lightly touched his tail, and he has opened his jaws to devour me and my brethren together. But his hour has not yet come, because as yet the Lord has not, through me and my brethren, wrenched from his jaws those whom He has predestined to the life of glory, for which He fills the heralds of the Gospel with firmness, that they may at least trample on Behemoth's tail until his head, with his other members, shall at length be fully crushed.

'This we accept with all our heart, for this we work as you, dearly beloved, have written. Therefore, as you write, we must endure death submissively, and we dare not, looking to the aid of the Lord Almighty, forget the thought which the supreme Lord expresses—"I will be with him in trouble, I will deliver him and glorify him." O holiest exaltation and glory! May you await Richard and his brethren, who have endured already much trouble. Accept poor me also, that I may be with my brethren, who acknowledge Thy law unshrinkingly in the midst of a corrupt and lying generation. Deliver us from trouble, for vain is the help of man. In Thee shall be our hope. Let the three-fold cord draw us to Thyself, that which cannot be broken because the Lord

Jesus Christ has prepared it. May He, dear brother, accord to you and your helpers life in untroubled glory, that you may be able to live long and bring back wandering sheep into the way of truth.

'It has been cause of joy to me and to all of us who love the Gospel that you, dearly beloved, have shown yourself so full of goodness to us, giving us such saving instruction. Our Lord the King, all his Court, the Queen, and the common people are interested in the word of Jesus Christ. The Church of Christ in Bohemia salutes the Church of Christ in England, desiring to be a sharer in the confession of the Holy Faith in the love of the Lord Jesus Christ. May the glorious God reward you for having in so great a matter given an example to us poor people. May the peace which passeth all understanding be with you. Amen.'

We took a sketch of the exterior of Hus's birthplace, and then once more we drove on towards Winterberg. Ere we reached this place, lying in the spurs of the Bohemian mountains, we saw ahead, over where the town lay, a wall of indigo black clouds slowly rising, vivid lightning darted amidst it. We were within sight of the town, the coachman whipped up his horses to try and reach the inn. The black wall swiftly mounted up, and seemed to bring on night, terrific peals of thunder crashed above us, and the lightning was terrible in its intensity; we dashed into the town, and as the first great flakes of rain fell turned into the inn courtyard. Night seemed to fall, when a blaze of flame seemed to light the room, and with it came a rattling crash. Hardly had its continuous echoing died away before the intense silence was broken by quick bugle calls, and cries of fire, quickly followed by shouts of '*Hochwasser! Hochwasser!*' floods! and we saw men hastening along the streets in the sheets of rain. Ere the torrents quite ceased we hastened out, to find all bridges over the narrow stream were being slung and chained to great trees; all furniture in lower rooms removed; all cattle got out of the stream-bordering meadows, and soon the little mountain thin streamlets were white and yellow-foaming cataracts. Down leapt the waters, carrying with them fields of crops, soon making the little rivulet a broad white flood of rushing, seething waters. Still it rose, until the steep-arched bridge, that had been high above the waters, was filled with the rushing, tossing flood, and all the wide meadows were a great lake; then, when the worst danger seemed to threaten, the rising ceased, the tumultuous flood rose no higher, and ere an hour was over the clear blue sky and hot sun reigned over this swiftly-risen, swiftly-falling flood, that had given us an exciting scene of life in these mountain towns.

In Bohemia, the lines of nationality and of costume are sharply drawn through certain districts. On nearing the famous district of Taus, where the costume worn is one of the most brilliant in all Bohemia, one expects to meet with at least isolated examples of the dress; but we were disappointed to find that in Klattau there was but little richness of costume, though, as throughout Bohemia, the women seemed instinctively to understand how colours will harmonise and contrast.

The most effective scene in Klattau is the corner of the square, where are grouped together the towers of the cathedral and the great tower of

the Rathhaus, known as the Black Tower from its colour, and in contradistinction to the White Tower that stands near the opposite corner of the square. Upon this Black Tower are two clocks, the lower one having the hours numbered in the old Bohemian fashion of one to twenty-four. An illustration of the square is given on page 131. Alongside the Rathhaus runs the great Jesuit College in the usual Renaissance style, with niches for saints; but the only saints to be seen now are the figures of soldiers leaning out of the windows; for, as elsewhere in Bohemia, the Jesuits' abode has become a commodious barrack. In the church adjoining the college are some very fair frescoes, the dome especially is a clever arrangement of perspective, giving the idea of classic arcading; and over the west door, but in a very bad light, is a good picture by Skrèta of Christ teaching in the Temple.

Here also one cannot help noticing how plain and simple are the decorations of the altars; but in the Dechanal Church, on the other side of the square, there are numerous gilt shrines and pictures. When we entered this latter church on a Sunday afternoon, it was crowded with worshippers; but how curiously did the people act in their behaviour in this Roman Catholic church! No reverence or genuflexion was made at the centre of

A WOMAN OF KLATTAU DISTRICT.

the church when the altar was passed. Boys knelt or lolled along the altar rails, but all joined heartily in the hymns and responses that were in

Cech, their own tongue. Men and women were mixed on either side, and not separated ; the music, with good organ and fine band, was excellent, and the peculiar subdued tone of colour of the women's headdresses helped to make the whole scene impressive and full of artistic beauty. Subdued blues and soft dull greens, dark reds, and soft browns, and dark purples were the colours loved by the women in this town ; hardly what we expected so near Taus.

The whole life of a Bohemian town centres in and around its Ring or Square. Here the people chaffer in the market, enter from it the house of God, setting down their burdens from their backs by the church door ; around its arcades are the inns where bargains are sealed and politics talked of, in subdued tones ; and in the *Zweites Zimmer* (second room) of the inn the clubs of the cultured classes read their papers and debate more freely literature and politics. In the Ring also is generally the Museum, and the Town Hall with its Justice Chambers, and its hall, where marriages are civilly sealed.

Klattau, as other Bohemian towns, has its well-ordered little museum, embodying a history of the town and the district, and hereby setting an example to many a far larger and more important English town. In every museum in Bohemia there is always a good collection of fifteenth and six-teenth century Bohemian books. The printing press was busy very early in its career in Bohemia, and Klattau has some rare Psalters and Bibles and missals on parchment and on paper, written and printed ; and here was arranged also an illustrative collection of prehistoric stone and jade and bronze and horn tools ; and not far off a collection of the costumes only lately worn, of gold and silver head-dresses, and brilliant-coloured bodices, now displaced by the soft dull colours we have seen in the church. One curious map of Bohemia of 1518 was printed with the top for south, and the bottom for north. The various privileges granted to the town, the old freedom and apprentices' indentures preserved here, give an excellent insight into the past life of this district.

At one time the town was in the hands of the Turks, and standing in the little park is an old solid round tower still called the Turk's Tower. There were seven of these towers, but now only four are left, and some goodly portions of the walls of the town can still be seen. The old inn of the Weissen Rose (White Rose) commemorates the fact that Kaiser Joseph rested here in 1771, by keeping his room most elegantly furnished, and having the royal arms and the date of his visit in relief on the ceilings. As an illustration of the type of German used here, we may note that *Metken* equalled *Mädchen*. One of these *Metken* sat for her portrait to an artist friend.

To those who have plenty of time and would study the Bohemian folk closely, as a change from driving, we can recommend taking what are called

From a drawing]   THE GATEWAY AT TAUS.   [by H. Whatley.

Bianco or white third-class ticket for a circular tour. These are excessively cheap. Our tickets cost us for a journey of about two hundred miles 2·96 gulden, or about five shillings; but it must be remembered that the trains are few and slow on these cross lines. The tickets can be purchased of agents in the various towns, and used when wished, but the breaks in the journey must be indorsed by the stationmaster where the break is made.

The country between Klattau and Taus or Domažlice (to give the Cech name that is used by the residents of the district) is very lovely, and marvellously cultivated; and we soon had glimpses of more brilliant costumes than we had seen at Klattau. We entered Taus beneath the old narrow high towered gateway of the town. A fresco over the arch depicting the arms of the town; two high-roofed towers rising above an embattled wall, below which are two swung open gates with portcullis half dropped; and above, between the towers, stands the protecting angel with drawn sword defending the town.

From a drawing]   GERMAN PEASANTS NEAR KLATTAU.   *[by H. Whatley.*

We drove on up the narrow Ring with quaint old houses on either hand, one side being arcaded, to the old inn of the Schwarzen Ross.

Our first pilgrimage from Taus was over the fields to the height upon the plain over the town where the great defeat by the Hussites of the Crusaders or Romanists under Cardinal Julian took place August 14, 1431.

L.

We passed through the little park or garden, and went on, with the high St. Laurence Hill, chapel-crowned, on our left. We had procured a German-

TAUS COSTUMES.

speaking man as guide, who pointed out the surrounding mountains and valleys to us as we struck northwards, with to west and south of us great

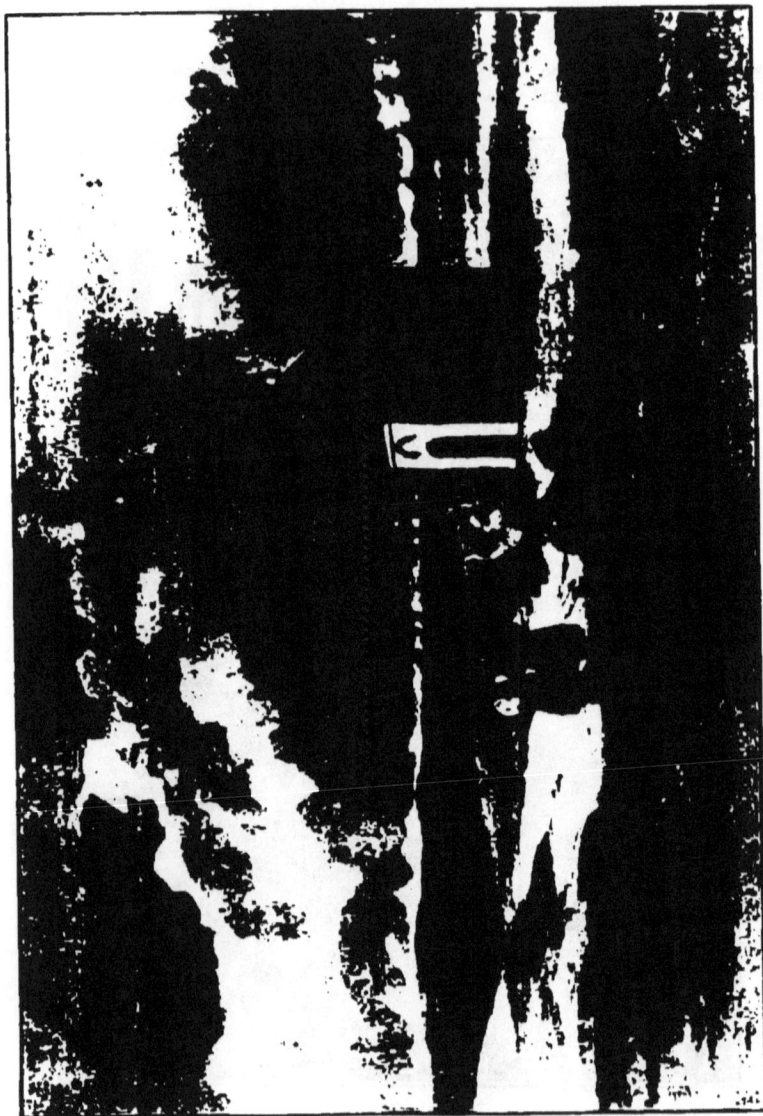

From a Drawing.   BALLOON IN CHAINS.   By H. P. Wells

lines of mountains, the peaks and ranges of the Böhmerwald. As we went on we saw approaching us two magnificent women, nearly six feet in height, walking with a proud free air, and dressed in a most gorgeous and picturesque dress. A black head-dress with long coloured ribbon streamers, a short dress, and aprons of various tones of red, a perfect study of various shades; high boots, and stockings also of a red tone. The proud, stalwart bearing of these women was very noticeable, and we asked from what village they came, and were told Luzenic, not far from the height for which we were making.

We soon caught sight of the little chapel on the high plain that was erected nearly five hundred years ago to commemorate the Hussite victory. We went across to it, and as we drew near its solid walls, three peasant women in brilliant costume drew near; and as we stood aside they halted before the door of the little chapel, and bowed their heads in prayer. Their costume was as brilliant as those we had met in the valley, but different. A red and black tartan head-dress, a blue jacket, and dark red tartan dress, with red stockings—the same brilliancy of colour, but yet a difference; and as the three women stood and prayed before this chapel on the hill plain, how picturesque and full of thought matter was the scene! We asked one man why the chapel was built. 'Oh,' he replied, 'it has stood here for four or five hundred years; there was a battle here.' And its thick sexagon walls, surmounted with a double-armed cross, looked solid enough to stand for another five hundred years.

So the flight of Cardinal Julian and his army of thirteen thousand Crusaders from the waggon forts, and fierce novel war tactics of the Hussites, was remembered; for our friend pointed out to us, to the south-east, the black height of Riesenberg, towards which the Crusaders fled. Still farther away, the twin peaks were seen beyond Newern, that rise above the Black Lake at Eisenstein.

A lovely panorama lay all round this historic hill: to the west the hills rise also, but not so high, and in this direction we can trace the two frontier roads that lead between the mountains from Bavaria, the roads by which the Crusaders entered Bohemia, and the roads over which the Choden, or watchers of the frontier, had to keep watch; for it was at Taus in the Chodenburg that this special race held their headquarters, and from them are descended the fine race of people · who still wear the Choden costume. These Choden, who adopted as their sign or arms the head of a sleuth-hound, were first appointed by Bretislaus I.; some historians say a guard of Poles, others merely a chosen band of the most faithful Bohemians. They lived here on the frontier at Taus, answerable to no overlord, and amenable to no laws but their own code and the king's command.[1]

[1] Those who are interested in such a phase of border history can learn more of their order and of their work in a monograph entitled, *Die Choden su Taus*, published by Brockhaus of Leipzig.

We lingered long over the Baldower Chapel and the view to be had from its height, ere we descended across the fields to Luzenic. Within the tiny chapel was a niche between two deep windows, with a picture of the Trinity: Christ with a cross at His feet, the Father as an old man with a curious rod, and the Holy Spirit as a dove, from whence rays of light proceeded. Four votive plaques were hung up, and 'Holy Jan' written up in several places. Probably, from the five-pointed cross outside, meaning Jan of Nepomuc, succeeding to Jan of Husinec (John Hus), who for two hundred years was regarded as a saint.

A STANDARD-BEARER OF THE CHODEN.

We left the height at last, and on entering the village of Luzenic found the little inn locked up; but the key was found, and whilst waiting for the landlord two little children crept in in quaint coloured clothes, that our artist friend sketched. The one, with a doll dressed in dark red like herself, in a doll's bedstead, the other already with a toy *hutte*, or pannier, on her back, training her to her life of toil and labour.

On the morrow, when we went into the museum in Taus, which is established in the handsome new Rathhaus, we saw examples of the dress for bridal and other *fête* days; and we were told by our good friend, Mr. Alex St. Halik, that the peasants had different colours for various occasions. On Church fast days they wore blue, on *fête* days red; for death, black, alternating with blue. The men wore long white coats, with blue stockings and broad hats, but they were fast giving up the dress, only a few men were left, as the old standard-bearer, and the musician who still clung to it.

In the Taus Museum are some interesting collections of important prehistoric finds. Amongst the coins are some Hussite Halire, or Hellers, the

name again given to the new 1893 coinage of Bohemia; over the inscribing
of which there has been a division as to what language should be used,
Cech or German.   This has ended in the curious compromise of no word
being placed on the coins, only a figure ten or twenty, and the Austrian
eagle.   Amongst the documents is a letter of Zizka's, probably a dictated
one, as the writing is so good; it commences with, 'Salute in the name of

CHILDREN OF LUZENIC.

Jesus Christ,' and is about some goods left in Taus by a lady of Gutstein,
not improbably a relative of the capturer of Peter Payne, and Zizka commands that these goods be given up to the lady.   How strange it is in
these museums to talk with men who are Roman Catholics, and yet
enthusiasts about Hus and Zizka, and all the mighty struggle of Bohemia
against Papal oppression!   The crushing of the Bohemian race at the battle
of the White Mountain all execrate.   'Then,' we heard one lover of his

country exclaim, 'we lost all. We were rich, powerful, learned; the greatest German University was in Prague, but then we lost everything. The good of the Reformation, the freedom of thought; then every woman knew her Bible;' and yet he who spoke was a Roman Catholic.

A most interesting relic of local village rule, that reminded us of how our own English Parliament has grown from such rule, and still preserves some of its old customs, was the 'Right' staff of the town or village Burger-meister or Mayor. It is a short twisted staff of gut or leather. The head of the village or town bore this into the room where council was to be held, and when he laid it on the table all must be silent. Exactly as 'that bauble' is laid on the table of the House of Commons when the House is sitting. And if old custom and ancient rights and old-world life can be studied in Taus, so also can modern industrial life be seen here; for some of the factories in the district are large, and the field cultivation is most excellent.

In company with our energetic friend we drove out to visit the old ruins of Herren, or Herstein, and Riesenburg. These were two of the border castles built to defend the frontier.

Riesenburg, which readers of George Sand's *Consuelo* will remember, has a ruined wall with a great double embankment round it, and outer towers, one with an underground passage. The centre tower has been restored by Count Stadion, and climbing this we looked out over a wide panorama, a very lovely scene. Tiny Taus lay with its great, high, round tower nestled in the hollow; we could see the Porta Terra, or land pass, the Choden had to guard, the pass to which the Crusaders fled, and all the range of the Böhmerwald; and to the north the deep black hills and great plains away to Pilsen, from whence the Hussites marched on to the invading Crusaders with their chant of 'Ye who are God's warriors.' This Riesenburg was in possession of the Crusaders, but when they knew of the defeat beyond Taus, they too, though numbering 4000, hastened out of the country.

In no country have we ever met with such eagerness on the part of its cultured inhabitants to assist and give pleasure to anyone studying the history of their land, as in Bohemia. Here in Taus, on the evening after our drive, many assembled at the hotel to give us welcome and information, and photographs or sketches to help us in our work. The following morning being St. Mark's Day, was a *Bettag*, or praying day, and one appointed for the procession to bless the fields; so that at six o'clock we were astir, and at seven the great bells clanged forth from the Marienkirche, and hasting to it we saw most wondrous and gorgeous groups assembling. The church itself has but a little left in its north chapel and door of its old foundation; this little is of fourteenth-century work, the rest is all of the Jesuit rococo type; but outside the church, by the great high watch-tower, the scene was most brilliant. Here at the crucifix, by the church door, came and knelt groups of peasant women and girls, some with white head-

SOUTH BOHEMIAN COSTUMES.

dresses, others with black with deep blue jackets, red, many quilted short skirts, with brilliant woven and worked borders. Aprons of other hues—red and yellow. A varied, brilliant-coloured little shawl is wound over the breast, that with the mothers is very full, for as proof of their maternity each one wears a little down pillow or bed upon the bosom, and the shawl is tied with a knot of many coloured ribbons.

The scene in the church when full was very operatic, and after the short service was over, out came the procession; the schools first in dull ugly modern costume, then two acolytes, then banners and a great crucifix,

PROCESSION TO BLESS FIELDS—FIRST PRAYING STATION.

followed by three priests in purple robes adorned with silver and gold; then came a crowd of men mostly in modern dress, and then the long crowd of women in every conceivable hue. The men were fine tall stalwart fellows, and one of their number read the lines of the hymn they were chanting. Out through the town this bright procession wound, until just beyond where the town gate formerly stood at a little shrine all halted, and the priest read the Gospel; the children in the meantime, a little distance off, were singing a Bohemian hymn to a tune centuries old. Then the whole mass of people sang a hymn, and the priest offered a prayer for the fruitfulness of the seed, and that it might come again good into the house; then the whole mass of colour sunk down in the roadway, and all with low earnest voices said the Lord's Prayer. Most pathetic and full of meaning was the scene, with the cultivated hills tilled by this praying crowd all around, the flowering fruit-trees stretching away, and the chestnut-trees above them just bursting into leaf. Five times the Lord's Prayer was said in their own tongue—all the service was in Cech—and then the procession wound on again out over the fields, to halt at certain spots and pray for God's blessing on their toil, and for fruitfulness of their fields.

As we drove away from Taus, making a halt at the little cemetery to look at the church standing in it, which is of the Decorated period, we felt that this one scene alone would repay any lover of the picturesque or beautiful, or any student of ethnology or history, for his journey to Taus. And yet had we not seen much more of beauty and of interest in and around its borders?

And it was from Taus by way of Klattau that we made our excursion to Burg Rabi, a famous old castle, now a proud ruin of noble proportions. From within its first court can be seen two great square keeps and four towers to the north. Round to the western side are the great trenches of rock and mounds within the great outer wall, that is twenty feet thick.

From above the south walls one can look out over the little village of Sichovic, or Schicowitz, with the Ottawa winding amidst the cottages and fields; and beyond the wide plain the heights of the Bohemian mountains to the south. The second court of soft greensward is surrounded with halls and chapels, and two great Hunger Towers; and the third court is but a narrow deep ravine between solid rock, on which is perched the innermost keep. On the north side is the great door, hid and protected from missiles by a massive blind wall; some pointed doorways are left, and some traces of windows, and the stone-work is interlaced with brick in almost Roman fashion in some parts.

The castle is, in spite of its ruin, a mighty pile of masonry, and still speaks of its power when Zizka besieged it in 1420. It was considered impregnable, and to look at it now in ruin one marvels how it could be stormed. Nobles and priests had sent all their jewels, and gold and silver, and costly garments here for safe custody, but Zizka stormed it, and his warriors piled treasure and dresses in a heap, and burnt them in company with seven monks and priests who had taken refuge here. But Rabi had its revenge upon Zizka, for it again came into the hands of Sigmund's party, and when in 1421 Zizka again besieged it, an arrow glancing from a pear-tree pierced the eye still left to him. A Prague doctor drew the arrow from his eye, but could not restore his sight; but nevertheless he continued the siege, and again captured the castle, and also the great leader of the Papal party, Meinhardt of Neuhaus. This is the most striking episode in Rabi's history; its archives, alas, were burnt.

WOMEN AT THE FOUNTAIN, Many

NEPOMUC.

CHAPTER X.

FASHIONABLE BOHEMIA: MARIENBAD, EGER, AND CARLSBAD.

WE must make our way back again to Taus, making a halt at
Nepomuc to see the birthplace of John of Nepomuc, and thence
across, viâ Pilsen, to Mies; and Nepomuc is within easy distance of Pribram.

We are fast approaching the fashionable cosmopolitan part of Bohemia
that all the world knows, the Baths of Marienbad, Carlsbad, Franzensbad,
where English tourists congregate, and the American accent is heard; but
at Mies we are still in 'undiscovered Bohemia,' where life is simple and
labour is strenuous, men working even in mines for about tenpence a day
of twelve hours. Here, curiously enough, even field labour is better paid, men
earning one shilling to one and twopence per day; but bread is fairly cheap
here, rather under a penny a pound, and the peasant and artisan live on bread
and potatoes and coffee. So five shillings a week is a 'living wage'; but the
pit men die young, and the women's dress of many petticoats in the extreme

cold, but all of linen, flannel being rarely worn, is with their hard labour conducive to premature age.

Mies has not the mediæval appearance of some of the towns we have been visiting, but as at Monmouth the gate at the bridge still stands, with its spire-like tower forming a picturesque object as we reach the bridge over the Mze, and look up to where some portions of the walls still stand with the clustering houses overtopped by the high square dome and open turret surmounted church tower.   The bridge gate tower is of sixteenth-century work, but the church of the Minorites goes back to 1253, and the town itself was founded, as portrayed in a fresco on the picturesque Renaissance Town Hall, in 1131.   This Town Hall at the end of the Ring-platz is a richly decorated example of Renaissance architecture.   Black and white frescoes adorn its triple pinnacled gables and façade.   Symbolical and allegorical figures and scenes from the history of the town are intertwined with rich scroll-work, and the whole effect is good.   One fresco depicts the defence of the walls in 1427, when the great crusade under Henry, Bishop of Winchester, was sent by Pope Martin V. to crush the heretic Hussites. Before Henry joined his enormous force, a letter was sent to Ulrich of Rosenberg saying the Crusaders were encamped in the best order before Mies, and all went well.   'Much of the walls of the town had been destroyed, and there was hope they would storm the town in the following week.' But the men of Mies gave a good account of themselves, and when Henry of Winchester joined his army, Prokop with his waggon forts had drawn near, and the great crusading army of, according to the lowest estimate, some 80,000 men was in full retreat, and the siege of Mies was abandoned.   This was on August the second, and on the fourth they reformed in battle array at Tachau, nearer the German frontier; but on the approach of Prokop a panic seized the Crusaders ; Henry of Winchester, with his 1000 English archers, was present, he stormed and raged against the fleeing papal troops, but soon had to save himself by flight, and these events, in which our own countrymen took part on both sides, for Peter Payne was the spiritual adviser with Prokop of the Hussites, are now depicted on this interesting Town Hall of Mies.

Our principal object in visiting the town was to drive out to the mountain castle Gutenstein, where Johann Burian of Gutenstein held Peter Payne prisoner whilst he corresponded with the Pope and Henry VII. of England, in hopes of getting a good round sum for the delivery of the body of the heretic dead or alive.   The entrance to Gutenstein is a square cellar or magazine cut in the rock, then, beyond, a level court, the rock cut away to obtain this.   Within this is another court with a vallum running across, and all around are ruins of great halls and rooms, and the high great tower far above all, still intact in its solid strength.   Working round to the tower, we found it defended where the land sloped by a thick outer wall, and

MTES.

M

beyond by a craggy fall of rock some fifty feet down on one side. East-
ward were three holes, attempts to enter or storm it; one had pierced it,
and by lying down and wriggling through the about fifteen feet of wall we
got inside this tower: narrow at the bottom and widening at the top. Here
only three storeys could be seen; the upper one a fairly wide room, but

GUTENSTEIN CASTLE.

where we stood it was only about eight feet by five in measurement. Again
wriggling out, we passed round to the south side of the tower; here, in a
good room, started up a pine, shadowing the walls of these apartments,
which rose up in three low storeys, having formed rooms about twenty-two
feet by fifteen. From here the height and strength of the tower could be
seen. It was square, but with wide rounded corners—an unusual type

M 2

of building; it rose to about eighty feet in height, and on its summit from the walls grew a fair-sized tree. To the south-east of this line of apartments was what appeared to be the great hall, the windows of which to the south were deeply splayed and narrow. To the south an outer wall gave a good view down into the valley some 150 feet below.

Leaving the old walls on the south-east, we found a wide sloping path, probably the horse-track, leading down to the Hadowka river; but in a moment all trace of the castle was lost, and no sight of its walls could be seen behind the grand old pines that filled the valley, through which ran the little river rippling over a wooden weir, where a green meadow sloped between the hill-sides. Here was that strange silence of the forest, unbroken by the sigh of the wind in the upper pines, but increased by the burst now and then of a song-bird's trill or cheep, as it flew from tree to tree or rested for a moment. Winding along by the river we could see this old robber-nest was isolated on its craggy peak save at one side, and on that side a vallum defended its entrance. As we strolled on alone we wondered if Peter Payne had been allowed by the robber-knight Burian to wander down here by the little river's brink; or if he awaited the replies of those letters from Pope and King of England within that dark tower's dungeon, dreaming of Oxford and Lincolnshire, of his home at Hough-on-the-Hill, and all his young life that he had left behind him for truth's and freedom's sake, to fight on here in distant Bohemia Wyclif's cause. Many months he must have lain here, until his friends, the Bohemian Wyclifites, paid his heavy ransom.

Gutenstein being a not uncommon name, there was a doubt when we first decided to visit this ruin as to whether this was the actual castle where Peter Payne was imprisoned, and awaited the news of his welcome ransom; but in the famous illustrated work on Bohemia called *Cechy* we met with this passage, which positively sets all doubt at rest:

'The castle Guttenstein we find in the thirteenth century in the possession of the Lords of Krasov, who in the fourteenth century were known as "von Guttenstein," *i.e.* ennobled; at first they were known as "Puta," being only knights. In the fifteenth century the family had become rich, and played an important *rôle* in history. During the Hussite war, the castle was in the hands of Burian of Gutstein, one of the leading lords of the Catholic party, who took an active part in all battles and discussions. In the year 1448, however, Burian went over, as did so many Bohemian nobles, to George of Podiebrad, and remained faithful to King George until his death.'

This short extract is conclusive that here Peter Payne was imprisoned by his capturer Burian, whose letters to Henry of England and the Pope luckily Bishop Beckington has preserved for us; and now, after a lapse of nearly five hundred years, Peter Payne takes his place in English history as one of the great reformers—the English link between Wyclif and Luther. As we drove back to Mies from Gutenstein we felt thankful we had been able to trace out and visit the walls of his old prison in this beautiful and romantic valley.

The sagas and legends that cling in the minds of the peasantry about these robber-nests on these mountain solitudes are rich in touches of fierceness and pathos, of daring and of tender solicitude and love ; and generally crime and hatred and cruelty are dogged by Nemesis, and receive their payment in full. A book on Bohemia would not be complete without at least one of these legends that so richly illustrate the wild life led in these castles ; and one that we heard told of the Castle of Tollenstein, that we passed in driving through Northern Bohemia, will form a sharp contrast to the fashionable nineteenth-century life in Marienbad and Carlsbad, and so, ere entering these towns, we tell the story here of The Seven Brothers of Tollenstein. Long years ago there lived on the Tollenstein an aged knight who had seven sons. But in the castle rarely reigned even a moment's joy, for the cruel old knight held his sons in with a tight rein, until at last the spirit of revolt, combined with avarice (for the old father's vast treasure was entirely withheld from them), fanned their duty into hatred, and they plotted together, and at length bound themselves to slay their father on the first opportunity, to take possession of the castle, to divide the treasure, and so live in pleasure after their own minds. Soon a plan was concocted and adopted to carry out this crime without exciting any suspicion. As on a certain day the old knight was going forth alone hunting, the sons armed themselves as usual, each left the castle on various errands, taking different routes, but when beyond the circuit of the castle each doubled back, and all met at a rendezvous, fell upon their father in the deepest part of the forest, slew him, and buried the body within a close thicket. Then binding themselves with an oath never to reveal the deed, they separated, agreeing that each should return to the castle by the various routes by which they had left it in the morning ; but not until the evening were they to enter the castle, now theirs through the murder of a father.

Now the youngest of these brothers was the wickedest of them all, and he determined to turn this crime to his own sole advantage ; so he hastened back straightway to the castle, called all the retainers together, and in piteous tones told them how his brothers had slain their father, and attempted to take his own life, but he had by a miracle escaped from their swords, red from a father's blood. He entreated them with prayerful words to save him from his bloodthirsty brothers. Horror-stricken, the retainers heard the words of the young knight, swore fealty to him, hastened to draw the bolts and shoot the great bars across the castle gates, to be prepared for any surprise.

When evening fell in gentle peacefulness, the six brothers appeared before the gates, but only to hear the cry from the ramparts, of, ' Flee, father-murderers ! ' and in vain they attempted to assert their innocence.

The warders on the walls would not listen to their words, but hurled great stones upon them, that fell clattering upon their armour and upon their prancing steeds. They demanded that the great doors should be swung open, but had for answer a shower of bolts and arrows, that proved to them they had been betrayed; and with rage and cursing they fled from the walls.

But the betrayed brothers were not content to so lightly let go their rich booty and inheritance. They hastened to the neighbouring castles, told of the bloody death of their father at the hand of their brother, cried aloud for revenge on the cruel deed, and prayed to the neighbouring knights for help against the murderer. Soon they rode forth to Tollenstein with a powerful force to aid them in its capture. Long and fierce was the siege, and determined and desperate the defence. The besiegers called aloud to the men on the walls, and denounced the youngest son as the real murderer. Bit by bit, they obtained a better heeding, until at length the besieged began to feel mistrust in their leader. He fought bravely at their head, and they dared not forsake him; but one day a bolt pierced his armour, and he could no longer walk the galleries of the ramparts, and urge on his men. And then the mistrust and doubt increased, and with growing dread and horror he saw his men, as they came into his chamber, look upon him with black and horror-stricken looks. They began to whisper amongst themselves, and he knew the defence was being carried on listlessly and half-heartedly. Darker and darker grew the brows of his most trusted followers, and whisperings grew to mutterings, and he feared the worst, and in his conscience-stricken terror determined to flee the castle. As soon as his wound was nearly healed, on a black stormy night he crept down into the cellar, opened a cask of the oldest and most famous wine, and poured poison into it. Then creeping to other parts of the castle, he left firebrands to do their work, and then with one old retainer, who still trusted him, he escaped from the castle.

Soon, red flames lit up the black night clouds. The besiegers seized their ·opportunity, and attacked the walls threatened with flames within and with death without. The men searched for their leader, but he was nowhere to be found, and with death around them, and half-hearted in their cause, they drew back bars and bolts, let go drawbridge, and raised portcullis, and in streamed the six brothers and their armed followers. Quickly the flames were got under, and when this was accomplished the tables were spread, the best food from camp and castle was prepared, and that night they determined to feast and revel in the hardly-won castle, and to celebrate their victory. The choicest wine-cask that their old father loved was tapped, and ere midnight the castle hall rung with revelry and shouts of victory, as beaker clanged against beaker, and was emptied by the six brothers.

Without, in the black raging night, the youngest brother hastened on

MARIENBAD

through the dark forest; but the inflamed blood and hot passion had renewed the fever of his wound. He gasped and panted from thirst, and at length fell exhausted against a tree, and begged his follower to find him water. The old servant left to find brook or spring, but ere he had been gone a few moments the feverish knight fancied he heard the clatter of weapons, and in his terror and anguish he cried aloud to his follower to return to bear him deeper into the forest, for he was helpless.

None answered, and he strove to move, but in vain, and again he cried aloud, and soon a man appeared, took him on his shoulders, and bore him swiftly through the forest, urged on in his speed by the wounded knight, who dreaded to fall into his brothers' hands.

On went the man, but gave no answer, when suddenly they emerged from the forest, and before him the young murderer saw the castle, from whence still rang the noise of revelry.

'Oh, you are deceived!' he cried aloud; 'I would not return here.'

'But I would!' rang the terrible words. In terror the murderer looked upon him who bore him, and in the light of the moon that burst through the fleeing cloud masses he saw the spirit of his murdered father. The eyes looked upon him glassily from the pale forehead beneath the white hair, all bloody and matted. He shrieked aloud, and strove with desperate struggles to free himself, but in vain. On went his ghostly bearer with great strides up the steep mountain side, on up the last rocky height to the walls, on through the self-opening door, where terrified watchmen started back at the sight, on into the knight's banqueting-hall, where now, cramped in death agonies, moaned and writhed the six brothers, poisoned by the fatal wine. The next morning, when the retainers entered the knight's hall, they found the seven brothers lying upon the floor all dead.

In consonance with the quick changes of life in Bohemia, we plunge from this legend of life on these castled heights in the Middle Ages to the fashionable life in the baths of Bohemia of to-day. Marienbad, Franzensbad, Carlsbad, Teplitz, all lie close together along the north-west frontier of the country, and on the spurs of the Erzgebirge, in the midst of very beautiful mountain scenery. Marienbad lies nearly 2000 feet above the sea-level, and the air is deliciously light and pure, and one can walk very quickly from the fashionable promenades into the heart of pine forests, and drink in the health-giving resinous odour of the pines. And a residence in Marienbad, fairly early in the season, which begins on the first of May, is delightfully bracing. The stroll out in the early morning, the band playing from six to eight, the glass of water from the prescribed spring, and perchance the climb to one of the neighbouring heights, perhaps up to the tower-crowned height known as the Kaiserthurm, from whence a glorious panorama lies beneath one, gives a remarkably good appetite for breakfast, if your doctor will allow you to eat a substantial meal.

The chief promenade for those who cling to the town is between the
principal spring, the Kreuzbrunnen and the Karolinenbrunnen, a pleasant
Allee with gardens and bazaar well laid out. A German guide says plainly
that the waters of Marienbad are good for those who have lived 'not wisely,
but too well;' they are a cure for obesity and most diseases of the digestive
organs, for poverty of blood, and for all those states of the body that
conduce to hypochondriacal and pessimistic feelings.

Ere reaching Carlsbad, the most famous and most frequented of these
Bohemian baths, we must make a short halt at Eger. Although it is by no
means an inviting town to stay at, yet its castle and its historical associations
compel a visit. Eger is a busy manufacturing town, and the entrance into
it down a wide, dirty, coal-black road with poor houses on either side, is
forbidding to the traveller, but should he enter the great Ring-platz on a
summer's evening when the sun is lowering and lighting up the deep reds
and dark tones of the high old houses, he will see a picturesque sight.

A good idea of town and castle is obtained by a walk round the town
to the theatre, and past the old walls of the town, about forty feet high,
with little round watch towers inside the walls, and the wooden gallery for
the watchman's patrol *in situ.* The wall can be seen where it has
run on, and crops up again beyond the towers, and so runs on down to the
river. As we cross over the great drawbridge, the old black Heathen Tower
rises before us in its solid strength, its little round-headed Romanesque
windows giving a date for its building. Beyond is the little double chapel,
being one chapel built above another. The lower of these chapels is good
Romanesque, and the ornamentation is very rich, of the billet and zigzag
type. The pillars are decorated with good scroll-work and with well-carved
grapes at the corners of the capitals. The upper chapel has some pretty
pillars of marble, two round and two octagonal, the latter with figures of
devils and angels on the capitals, and the round pillars with foliage and
Byzantine scroll decorations. Close to this interesting chapel stands the ruins
of the great hall where Wallenstein's generals, Illo, Kinsky, and others were
murdered. Little is left of this but the arches to the windows, from whence
gleamed out the light that made Wallenstein demand of Gordon, when dis-
robing for the night in the Burgermeister's house :

'I hear the sounds of music, the castle is ablaze with lights. Who are
the jovial ones ?'

Gordon answers, 'A banquet is being given to Count Terzky (Tžcka)
and the Field-marshal.' The fatal banquet ended in blood.

In descending into the town from the castle the Church of St. Nicholas
should be visited. Its eight great round pillars, rising without capitals to the
spring of the roof-groining, are remarkable, and its long lancet windows and
double spires with pinnacles make it an interesting building. Next to the
castle, however, the spot in Eger that most haunts the visitor is the room

From a water-colour drawing)   THE BLACK TOWER AT EGER.   (by Walter Crane.

in which Wallenstein was murdered. This is the present Council House and Museum. Schiller in his tragedy calls it the Burgermeister's House. It stands on the Ring-platz, and from its doorway a good survey can be taken of the whole irregular Ring that has in past ages been filled with

A PROCESSION OF PATIENTS AT MARIENBAD.

Crusaders by no means burning to penetrate further into the land of Hussite and heretics, and in later centuries with Wallenstein's men-at-arms, and yet later, in 1742, with victorious Frenchmen. The high roofs and quaint gables of the houses, and some market-women in costume, aid the imagina-tion to step back in time and live again in turbulent days of mercenary war; and inside the museum is a room full of figures wearing the old costumes, and placed amidst the furniture and surroundings of an Egerland pea-sant's home, some old pictures of a peasant's wedding, etc., make this room of real interest, though much in the museum is childish.

The old courtyard, with its wooden gallery running round it, is filled with war relics and monu-ments, some of the fifteenth cen-tury, and some curious relics of bygone punishment; and much in-

A FAMILY PARTY AT CARLSBAD.

sight of past days can be gleaned here and in the history of Eger.

Carlsbad is the capital of the baths of Bohemia, but Carlsbad life is hardly Bohemian life; and yet what is termed 'Bohemian' life in England is very largely represented in Carlsbad, especially in the height of the season. There may be seen promenading in the 'Old Meadow' Bohemian people from every quarter of the globe. There is no meadow now to be seen, but interlaced lines of trees beside the bazaar-like shops give a pleasant soft shade from the hot sun that pours down into the rocky valley with great power. This promenade widens out into well-laid-out gardens, where, by a most excellent orchestra, the choicest music is given with inspiring force and delicacy. And for the early season, when the weather is not reliable, concerts are given in the glass halls of the Stadt Park or the Wells.

AT THE ALTEWEISE, CARLSBAD.

The well-built villas and great hotels stretch along in the deep rocky valley beside the rushing waters of the little Tepl River, and close beside its waters burst forth the great hot-springs of the Sprudel Markt and Muhlbrunnen and the other springs, that number fifteen in all. At the Sprudel the steam of the hot spring rushes out from the apertures below the new glass colonnade, where the patients patrol with glass in hand, and forces itself out of crannies by the side of the rocky bed of the little river. The fact that this spring pours forth over a hundred and fifty thousand quarts an hour is evidence of its strength. Here at six in the morning a concert begins, and at this hour patients may be seen who at home have probably lain a-bed until ten. The *régime* is very strict. Up before six, go to the spring advised, take a half pint of the water, and then patrol for twenty minutes, then another half pint and another patrol, so drinking four half-pints, and meditating on your former excesses for one hour. Then out of this glass and iron hall, that must become a hall of torment to many a patient, and a walk up some of the neighbouring heights for an hour, which brings the morning on to eight A.M. Then to breakfast, but only a very slight one, and during the day very little must be eaten, and no wine or beer drunk. What would such treatment do for many of our sickly ones on our own breezy downs and sea-breathed hillsides? But here at Carlsbad obedience to rule is well inculcated, and thereby many a life saved, and made healthy and happy.

There is gaiety enough at Carlsbad, but the *memento mori* is ever present at the gayest assembly in the presence of patients from all lands and of all tongues suffering from jaundice and obesity, and other digestive complaints in their fiercest forms. These, in the earlier days of their visit, cling to the level walks by the river's bed, but soon their obedience enables many to climb the rocky heights that close it in, and some glorious walks are all around Carlsbad. In the midsummer the heat is very great on these hill-slopes, but in early spring the soft fresh air is very invigorating, for the Erzgebirge that rise around are often snow-clad when Carlsbad lies in warm summer weather. The wind that pours down amidst the ravines with the Tepl stream, keep the valley temperate in the morning and evening even in August.

Above Carlsbad is a spot poetically named '*Das ewige Leben*,' Eternal Life, a beautiful look-out at all seasons of the year. Returning thence on one occasion, there came up to us the harmonious strains of a band, and winding up an opposite height we saw a long procession going on up over the white snow, a black banner unfurled before them, priests in white following, and then the coffin with lighted torches, and the long trailing funeral train—on upwards, they also, to *Das ewige Leben*. How sharp the contrast after such a scene to come down to a gay concert in the town with all the Cur guests crowding round, to the crash of light jovial music, and the light chatter of *insouciant* gaiety!

Drinking the waters as a cure commenced in 1520, but the first Curhaus was not erected until 1711, after the Emperor Joseph II. had raised Carlsbad to the rank of a royal free town. Now large numbers visit it annually as guests and patients for its waters, its gaiety, or its natural beauties. It is an easy place to approach or to get away from, for at Eger close at hand are lines branching to all parts of Europe, and the line on which it stands quickly runs one through charming scenery to the Elbe, and thence to the northern capitals of Europe.

THE DECHANAL CHURCH AT SAAZ.

CHAPTER XI.

SAAZ AND THE ELBE.

THE journey to Saaz from Carlsbad is very full of charming peeps of scenery. It passes the romantic Joachimsthal that gave its name to the money of Germany and America. The valley was rich in silver, and in 1517 one of the Schlik family coined here the first 'Thalers,' Joachimthalers that originated the word 'Dollar' in America. After passing this valley the rocky bed of the Eger is followed through a wild country of pines and rocks and ruin-crowned precipices ; but after Deutsch Kralup and Komotau a flatter country is entered, and as we near Saaz wide plains with far-reaching hop-fields stretch around us where the famous hops are grown that enrich the Saaz merchants.

Saaz lies on an isolated rocky plateau, and the view of it as we approach with towers and domes, and spires and fragments of its old walls

and watch-towers still standing, impresses one with its former strength and importance, and it was to a living in this town that the Englishman Peter Payne was appointed in the fifteenth century. It was in the Dechanal Church here that he preached, and where men who listened to him urging trust in the doctrines of Wyclif might in after life have listened to Luther's words in Wittenberg. Then the men of Saaz were warm Wyclifites and ardent Bohemians; now as we strolled about the town and chatted at the hotel or in the shops we found them German and Romanist. In 1421, six times the Crusaders stormed its walls, but the Saazmen were too much for them, and held the town until Zizka's advance alarmed the Papal troops and routed them; and after the battle of the White Mountain the town was Germanised, and so it remains to this day.

A walk round the town shows many portions of the walls and tower gates still well preserved. The Branka or Ausfall, *i.e.* Sortie Gate, is one of these, and the great Priester Gate is still the principal entrance to the town; the Water Tower is also preserved; beyond the Priest's Gate is a great platform of part of a castle now used as a brewery. In the Rathhaus that stands on the Ring-platz is a well-preserved plan of the town dated 1464, just nine years after the death of Peter Payne, and from this we can well judge its appearance and life at his time. The walls then encircled it with numerous towers and red pents, the tall Priest's Gate, and the Dechanal Church and Town Hall, and the steep Sortie Gate, were all then as now. The arms of the town are three towers beneath a crown.

After looking at this plan of the period we entered the Dechanal Church where so often Peter Payne had preached and advocated Wyclif's teachings. It was founded in 1206, and its high lancet windows spoke of the architecture we term Early English. It is of rather peculiar shape, a square nave supported with high round pillars, and with very slight aisles at the side, in fact, a square church with a deep chancel and apse with three windows. The pulpit now stands at the first north pillar in the nave. Did it stand there when Payne preached beneath this roof upheld by the six plain pillars with a plain beading at the top, from whence springs the roof groining? Neither town nor church was so wholly altered but we could call up a vision of this Englishman exiled from Oxford here holding fast to his great Master's teachings through scenes of terrible bloodshed and horror, through imprisonment and death dangers. We could see him passing through the narrow streets of this town loved and revered by the Bohemians, who spoke a strange tongue, but whose hearts he had won, ofttimes probably wandering round the walls and looking out westward over the plain towards England, that had driven him from her shores outlawed and with a price on his head, but whose king refused to have him back as prisoner, to be handed over to his enemies of Rome.

Such thoughts as these clung to us as we walked the streets of Saaz,

N 2

and as we went on again through well-kept gardens of fruit and vegetables
and hops, on through Brux and into Teplitz. What a contrast is there
between the life in such towns as Carlsbad and Teplitz and that of Saaz,
which we have here placed between them! Saaz, quiet, solid, full of
industrial and calm business life, thinking only of its own affairs, and with
no visitors save merchantmen to buy its hops or vegetables; whilst
Teplitz, as Carlsbad, is full of strangers, though on a lesser scale, and teeming
in the season with cosmopolitan life. But Teplitz has not the natural
beauties of Carlsbad, and being in an iron and coal district, its suburbs and

A VIEW NEAR TEPLITZ.

environs are very coally and black. The prettiest part of Teplitz lies
towards Prince Clari's castle-grounds. Teplitz will hardly detain the
traveller long, but the ascent of the Mileschauer can well be made from
here, and this 'Thunder Mountain,' to give it its other name, that rises some
2500 feet, is well worth a visit. We passed out of Teplitz through the
villages to Pilkau, and from here a very easy climb of three-quarters of an
hour brought us to the summit. Here an inn is established, with moss beds for
those who like to remain the night, and certainly the view demands a fairly
lengthy stay for its charm and beauty. To the east is a varied plain, well

THE 'THUNDER MOUNTAIN,' TEPLITZ.

cultivated, beyond, in dark gloom as we looked on the scene, a mountain range, to the south rise two ruin-crowned peaks, one with a single tower of Wostrey, and one reminding us of Bösig of Hasenberg. Around Wostrey start up ten peaked and curious hills, exactly as if forming the crater of a great volcano. To the south-west three ruined castles are in sight, and numerous peaks, some flat, others round or sharp. To the north is the same marvellous view of hundreds of peaks interspersed with villages and towns, whilst to the east is a glimpse of the Elbe at Czernezek, and beyond again it is seen between the hills with an island in its midst above Leitmeritz. To the north rises the great chain of the Erzgebrige, snow-clad to late spring, and round to the west the chain of the Mittelgebirge. In the plains are dark forest-tracts and numerous towns and villages, and Rumour says in clear weather Prague and even the Böhmerwald can be seen from this height. The circle of from sixty to one hundred miles embraced in the view alone repays one for a visit to Teplitz.

We have caught a glimpse of the Elbe again, by which we entered Bohemia, and a very short run indeed brings us across its waters to the busy town of Aussig on its banks, and although here we are almost in the Black Country of Bohemia, in the heart of the coal and iron district, we are also in a district that has witnessed epoch-making events in history. Aussig itself is dirty and noisy. Smoke and steam and coal-dust speak of its importance to the commerce of Bohemia, but a day can well be spent in its neighbourhood, and frequent steamboats on the Elbe or frequent trains easily allow the traveller to escape in the evening.

One of our principal objects in visiting Aussig for the third time was to pass over the battlefield where, in 1426, the Hussites won their first great triumphant victory over their enemy King Sigmund and the Saxon troops of his vassal, Prince Friedrich of Meissen. Was aught left of the period of this battle that was of such importance to Europe? We could hear of nought, but we started off on a hot sunny morning out through the long lines of factories and works that run far out from Aussig to the village of Prodlitz. This village, Předlic, is mentioned in Palacky's graphic account of this battle, so we were in the right direction of the field.

It was on Saturday, June 15, that the king's army of three columns joined and entered Bohemia. They numbered about 70,000 men, 3000 waggons, and 180 shooting engines, whilst the Hussites numbered only 25,000 men. These waggon-forts that Zizka had so well taught the Hussites how to use were solid, high-sided timber waggons linked together with great chains. If our English officers had learnt tactics of Zizka, we might not have had to mourn for the slain at Isandlana and elsewhere in Africa. From these waggons the heretics awaited the onslaught, fired in safety upon the Germans, and when they were near hooked them with their long hooks from their horses, or felled them with their flails and morning stars, and when the great army was in disorder they raised their battle-cry and their war-song, and fell upon the disordered Germans, that were soon fleeing and pleading for the quarter they had so haughtily refused.

Now after nearly five hundred years what should we trace on the scene of this victory? The village of Prodlitz we identified with Predlic, and as we walked through it we saw a full stream rushing down with trees on, either side. To the north before us, a conspicuous object from its loneliness,

AUSSIG ON THE ELBE.

rose the little church of St. Laurence, with white and red roof and square tower, and black dome with open bell-turret with, at the east end, another little open turret. One house we now saw stood near it. Naught else but sloping fields and a line of rounded hills to the east, running down to the plateau. The windows and buttresses of the church were of the fourteenth century architecture, and at its east end, ranged round its outer walls, were some most quaint monuments. One to Mehlena Schonfeltin von Pettentts, dated 1590, and another of 1600, and on both the dress of the period was minutely graved. Another stone dated 1570 was of a woman with her hand on the head of a little child. A farmer friend told us that the little rising hill behind his house is called Běhana, and was where the Hussite fight took place ; but it must have spread over the whole plateau, and that away where the hills met was Kulm. Thus we were standing upon and looking over the *terrain* of two great battles, that of the Hussites, and that of the Allies against Napoleon on the 29th and 30th of August, 1813, when the army of *La grande Nation* experienced one of those series of disasters that led on to Leipzig and Waterloo.

The points of beauty and of historic interest near Aussig are by no means exhausted by this walk out to the Běhánà and Kulm battlefields. The whole district is full of scenes of natural beauty of ruined-capped heights and of fields of study for ethnologist, historian, man of science, and the student of modern industry. By crossing over the Elbe on the railway bridge, a short walk up the river brings us to an avenue of ash-trees, and ahead

SCHRECKENSTEIN.

is one of the most grandly placed and still imposing castle-ruins on the Elbe—the Castle of Schreckenstein. Its towers and solid walls and bastions rear up on the high jutting precipice of rock that commands a great sharp bend of the stream. It is literally the key to the Upper Elbe, and he who owned it was master of the river traffic, and documentary evidence exists that it was rebuilt in 1310 by Knight Pešig of Strekow, who was granted the Elbe tolls by King Johann of Luxemburg. He who afterwards, as King of

Bohemia, fell at Crecy in 1346, and gave his motto, *Ich dien*, to our Prince of Wales. The castle afterwards passed into the hands of the Wartenbergs, and in 1601 into the Lobkovic family, who still own it.

Quite enough is left of the ruin to make it an interesting study to the architect and archæologist. Some good thirteenth-century work is traceable, and the chapel and tower and walls allow the whole building to be rebuilt in the mind's eye. The Hussites stormed it before passing on to their

LOBOSITZ.

great Aussig victory; but for its history and the legends that have been told about it by the peasant's tongue from age to age we have no space left.

On the waters of the Elbe we are quickly borne up to Lobositz, though against its rapid current. And the river, as we wind and twist amidst the closing in or receding mountains, offers most lovely vistas of scenes full of natural charm and idyllic beauty. Lobositz is a somewhat modern town now belonging to the Schwarzenbergs, whose castle is one of the principal buildings; but it is modern, for with nearly the whole of the town it was burnt down in 1809. The town lies in the centre of the great fruit district of the Elbe, and in the month of May all the sloping meadows around it are gay with cherry and apricot blossom, that contrasts delightfully with the green grass and the sombre yet winter russet pine and the soft emerald green of the fresh leaf of the birch. For 650 years Lobositz has been noted for its fruit; a document is extant of fruit sales in 1248.

Within sight of Lobositz on the opposite bank is Leitmeritz, where the steamboat journey ends. Bohemian energy should arrange for boats of lighter draught to continue the river journey on to Prague, and as we pass up the river on this last little stage, and look around from the river's bosom on to the high, varied, round, and jagged peaks or foliaged heights with ruined towers here and there, and peeps of distant mountain ranges, we feel that this surely is the most perfect of river and mountain scenery so varied in form and colour, with every variance of light and shadow, sunlit mountain-side or deepening depth of forest-clad valley, the air filled with song-birds' notes and cuckoos' call, or scream of small birds as some brown-feathered poised bird of prey threatens their life, the one note of cruelty in a scene of pastoral beauty that reminds us of all the horrors and bloodshed this glorious land has suffered.

And as we near Leitmeritz there rises up above the roofs of the town one of the most singular and expressive monuments that ever man devised. A tower in form as a cup or chalice, the great sign of freedom of the Wyclifites of Bohemia, and near it rises the curious peaked tower of the church, and beneath the two red domes of the Jesuit church. These two monuments tell of Bohemia's history, of her might as a European state, defying for two centuries the greatest power yet known on earth, and of her being crushed out of European nations, but now again risen to be a most important portion of the great Austrian Empire.

As we pass up from the landing-stage and enter the great square and look round on the quaint towers and building of Rathhaus and church, and watch the women crossing the vast space with their water pails on their backs, or their market loads, life goes back with us, and we are transported to the Middle Ages, and when we enter the inn and find our bedroom is a great sleeping-room where a company of troops might easily repose, we think of the strange bedfellows old mediæval days made travellers acquainted with, but are reassured when told the vast chamber is for two travellers only.

The great square echoes now but to the rattle of bullock waggons and market-carts and the laugh of children at play, but it has witnessed some of the most terrible scenes. Sigmund often made it his resting-place, and in May 1420, in the early days of the Hussite Wars, the then Burgomaster, Pichel, wishing to ingratiate himself into favour of the king, by the help of some of

the king's men, seized seventeen of the suspected burghers, bound them hand
and feet, and threw them into the Elbe. The tale lives in the minds of the
people, for from revenge or refined cruelty amongst those so seized was the
betrothed of his own daughter. All her tears or prayers and passionate
pleadings were of no avail, her lover was borne bound to the Elbe stream,
and before her eyes hurled in ; but she leaped after him, seized him in her
arms, and together in death the floods bore them from Leitmeritz.[1] Such
scenes were common enough in those days, but in May 1421, the Leit-
meritzers learnt that Zizka was approaching, and in terror they yielded to

LEITMERITZ, WITH THE CHALICE TOWER.

Prague, and Zizka desisted from the siege. From that time Leitmeritz
remained true to the Hussite cause. The Chalice House with its Cup Tower
was not built until the sixteenth century by a rich Utraquist burgher. Before
Leitmeritz yielded, Zizka had captured a castle near Triebisch, and refortifying
it, had named it Kelch, or Chalice, a name it bears to this day, an
interesting visit from Leitmeritz, with numberless walks around it.

The Chalice House is now a school and museum, and this and the
Rathhaus and cathedral, and the Dechanal and Jesuit churches, will well

---

[1] This incident is pathetically and forcefully interwoven into the story *Crushed yet Conquering*, by the author
of the *Spanish Brothers*, a story that well pictures the life of the period.

fill up a day in and around the great square of Leitmeritz, with much of history weaving itself into the day, for also in the seventeenth century, in the Thirty Years' War, did the town suffer for its faith, until most of its Protestant burghers were driven out and replaced by Catholic Germans.

There is a town not far from here we have missed, the town of Melnik,

GROTESQUE ROCKS, LIBOCH, NEAR MELNIK.

famous for its wine, and for the scenery and grotesque rocks in its neighbourhood.

Those who enter Bohemia by continuing up the Elbe to Leitmeritz, can strike into the Haida district, described in the early part of this work, by driving; but we must cross over the river to Theresienstadt, and take the train up to Raudnitz, to visit our last untouristed simple town, and to ring the sonorous bell at its castle gate, to summon the warder to open it. The town lies on a hill-side, and up on its slope is a straggling wide open place, and as we pass to the end of this we are watched by the women at the Brunnen, who halt from bearing or drawing water.

The castle is the one point of interest here; it is linked with the fortunes and fame of the Lobkowitz, Wallenstein, Wartenberg, and Thun families, and in 1350 a famous character in history was sent here by Carl IV., and left in the hands of the archbishop, 'to be taught and improved.' The teaching and improving of the fiery Cola di Rienzi, the tribune of the people of Rome, was carried out by the archbishop, by lodging Rienzi in the dungeons beneath this castle. And for a year he lay here, until the papal legate came with proof that Rienzi was a heretic, and bore him off to Avignon ; but Carl seems to have had a liking for Rienzi—or was it a dislike for the Pope?—at least he gave him safe protection from punishment for his past actions, and safety for his life.

From the balcony one looks out on to a wide stretch of country, with the wealth-giving silvery Elbe winding on between the mountains. Away to the west rises up the great Mileschauer, and before us the Geltsch, and to the right the Řip or Georgsberg. No one resides now for long in the castle, as the castellan said, 'Castle is too big, and the park too small for residence.' But it is kept in good order, and though this building was erected in 1650, yet its site and traditions, and the objects now gathered within it, bring before one Bohemia's march through the ages of European history.

And here, standing on this balcony looking out over this peaceful, wide-stretching landscape, where armed forces, from the earliest ages down to our own time of 1866, have marched and laid waste 'homestead and village, citadel and town,' here, from whence, within an hour, we can be far beyond Bohemia's borders, or in her heart—the city of Prague—we will say adieu to her fair landscapes, and her thrifty industrious peasantry, and her busy, intellectual and energetic townsfolk. The landscape before us speaks too of Bohemia's history ere yet history was begun, when fire and water and earthquake were moulding her hills, and her jewels, and all those documents of the past a geologist loves to contemplate ; and his brother scientist, the botanist, will look out to the Řip Mountain, and rest not until he has found some of the botanical rarities its slopes yield. From a local list we take *Ceterach officinarum, Scandix pecten Veneris, Muscari tenuiflorum,* and on the summit of the Řip—pronounced Chip—Mountain are to be found *Astragalgus austriacus* and *danicus, Hypericum elegans, Myosotis alpestris, Senecio campestris, Pulsatilla pratensis, Erysimum crepidifolium.* This will prove to the English botanist that he may find in Bohemia plants he might seek for in vain in our own country, and thus add an additional pleasure to his travels.

THE HOLY HILL AT PRIBRAM.

INDEX.

From a drawing]   ANCIENT CHAIR AT KUTTENBERG.   *[by H. Whatley.*

LONDON: PRINTED BY WILLIAM CLOWES AND SONS, LIMITED, STAMFORD STREET AND CHARING CROSS.